the Complete Instant Pot Cookbook

Over 1000 Every day Quick & Easy Foolproof Instant Pot Recipes for Beginners

Sophia Sanderson

Look Inside

Spicy Korean Cauliflower Bites

Prep Time	Cook Time	Serving
15 Minutes	30 Minutes	4

Ingredients

2 eggs
1 lb. cauliflower
2/3 cups of corn starch
2 teaspoon smoked paprika
1 teaspoon garlic grated
1 teaspoon ginger grated
1 lb. panko
1 teaspoon sea salt
For the Korean barbecue sauce:
1 cup ketchup
½ cup Korea chili flakes
¼ cup minced garlic
¼ cup red pepper

Directions

1. Cut the cauliflower into small sizes based on your taste and pre

2. In a small bowl add cornstarch and eggs and mix them until th

3. Add onions, garlic, ginger, smoked paprika and coat them wit

4. Apply some pressure so that the panko can stick and repeat t
cauliflower.

Nutrition:

Calories: 141
Fat: 12 g
Carbs: 23 g
Protein: 11 a
Chapte

Healthy 2 Ingredient Breakfast Cookies Cocoa and Berry Breakfast Bowl

Prep Time	Cook Time	Serving
4 Minutes	15 Minutes	1

Ingredients

1 ½ cup of quick oats
2 large ripe bananas
4 teaspoon peanut butter
1/3 cup crushed nuts of your choice
½ teaspoon pure vanilla extract
¼ cup shredded coconut

Directions

1. Preheat your oven to 350 degrees Fahrenheit.

2. Mash the bananas in a bowl and add the oats and mix them well to combine. Fold any optional add ins such as ¼ cup chocolate chips. You can add honey to taste.

3. Line your baking tray with parchment paper and drop one teaspoon of cookie dough per cookie into your tray. Press down with a metal spoon into the shape of the cookies.

4. Bake for 20 minutes depending on your oven or cook them until they are golden brown on top.

5. Remove and allow to cool before serving

Nutrition:

Calories 24
Carbohydrates 5g
Proteins 1g

Chicken Parmesan

Prep Time	Cook Time	Serving
20 Minutes	15 Minutes	4

Ingredients

¼ cup of avocado oil
¼ cup of almond flour
½ cup parmesan cheese, grated
½ cup of marinara sauce, sugar-free
¼ cup mozzarella cheese, shredded
2 eggs, beaten
2 teaspoon, Italian seasoning
3 oz. pork rinds, pulverized
4 lbs. chicken breasts, boneless & skinless
Sea salt & pepper, to taste

Directions

1. Preheat the oven to 450° Fahrenheit and grease a baking dish.

2. Place the beaten egg into one shallow dish. Place the almond flour in another In a third dish, combine the pork rinds, parmesan, and Italian seasoning and mix well.

3. Pat the chicken breasts dry and pound them down to about ½" thick.

4. Dredge the chicken in the almond flour, then coat in egg, then coat in crumb.

5. Heat a large sauté pan over medium-high heat and warm oil until shimmering.

6. Once the oil is hot, lay the breasts into the pan and do not move them until they've had a chance to cook. Cook for about two minutes, then flip as gently as possible (a fish spatula is perfect) then cook for two more. Remove the pan from the heat.

7. Place the breasts in the greased baking dish and top with marinara sauce and mozzarella cheese.

8. Bake for about 10 minutes.

9. Serve!

Nutrition:
Calories: 621 Cal
Fat: 24 g
Carbs: 6 g
Protein: 14 g
Fiber: 6 g

Avocado Caprese Crostini

Cook Time	Serving
20 Minutes	2

Directions

at your oven to 375 degrees Fahrenheit

e your baking sheet properly before spraying them on top with olive oil.

ur item of choice until they are well done or golden brown. Rub your th the cut side of garlic while they are still warm and you can season pepper and salt.

basil leaves on each side of bread and top up with tomato halves, es and bocconcini. Season it with pepper and salt.

t minutes and when the cheese starts to melt through remove and ic glaze before serving.

26

Sophia
SANDERSON

Sophia Sanderson 58 years old, she attended one of the best courses at La Cuisine de Marie-Blanche-France, in Paris, coming out with top marks.

Writer, cook and activist Sophia Sanderson is the author of several cookbooks.

She is an expert in many and different diets, she wanted to write them on paper by inventing, re-studying and taking inspiration from the wonderful recipes, her books are therefore the result of 8 years of work.

She is now the head cook in her successful restaurants, and with the help of her chef collaborators she brings tradition and innovation into their kitchens, and it is often the place where her recipes are born!

Harmony, precision and determination distinguish Sophia and her recipes.

Table Of Contents

Introduction

There are so many reasons as to why human beings gain weight. Before the need to lose weight arises, there must have been a weight gain already. Weight gain can come from several causes like; poor sleep, sedentary activities, eating a lot of processed foods, consumption of sugary foods, and lack of exercise. People also gain weight after childbirth (this is peculiar to women), alcohol intake, among other reasons. For males, many of the causes that lead to weight gain or obesity have nothing to do with willpower. Weight gain for men can be due to the following; kidney failure, food addiction, the use of certain medications and lots more. It is often very easy to gain weight than to lose but Optavia Diet has made it a bit simple to lose weight for both the male and female folk. It can be very difficult to stick to a diet plan in the quest for losing weight due to a very busy schedule or because some find it difficult to prepare two dinners: one for you (on a diet), and the other for your family members.

There are so many diets that claim to have long-term benefits to people. It is therefore important that you constantly do due diligence on what diet works and what diet offers short-term results. One of the How Nutritious Is Optavia Diet

diet regimens that you might want to consider is the Optavia Diet. The Optavia Diet is one of the hottest trends of the many diet regimens that are available in the market. It is designed for people who want to achieve long-term weight loss. Moreover, this diet is also celebrated as one of the best diets in the United States. Therefore, if you want to adopt this particular diet to enjoy its benefits, then this book will serve as your guide on what you need to know about the Optavia Diet.

The OPTAVIA brand is a dietary plan created by the Medifast group. The unique product is identical to the macronutrient quality contained in all other Medifast products. Apart from developing the OPTAVIA diet, the company has independent coaches who educate consumers on nutrition. The Optavia Diet brand is widely known as "Fuelings." It is often balanced with beef, veggie, and high protein entrée.

Many well-known names have appreciated the plan, which determines as to how many meals you should consume per day, while also offering those pre-packaged meals.

In this book, we'll talk about everything you need to know about Optavia Diet. This book allows you to have quick and easy meals during the day which you can also fit into a busy schedule. In addition, the lean and green recipes in this book can be enjoyed by the whole family, even if they are not on a diet. Therefore, you do not need to rack your brain about what to cook for dinner…

Optavia is a weight reduction or maintenance strategy that recommends eating a combination of bought, packaged food known as "fueling." These mini-meals that the company sells are designed to fill you full and help you lose weight to lean and green recipes (homemade). The Optavia diet is a regimen that offers three food programs from which you can choose: Optimal Weight 5 & 1 Method, Optimal Weight 4 & 2 & 1 Method, and Optimal Health 3 & 3 Program. The latter is oriented toward maintaining weight. Each schedule recommends consuming a certain amount of "Fuelings," which are prepackaged by Optavia brand snacks or meals. These diets provide more than the government's guideline; that 10-35 % of the total calories comes from protein.

Half of the Optavia's diet plan, or even more, is its "Fuelings"; including cereal, bars, cookies, shakes, and a few savory choices: like mashed potatoes and soup. These packaged foods have whey protein and soy protein as the first ingredient.

Optavia diet enhances weight loss through branded products known as "Fueling" while the homemade entrées are referred to as the "Lean and Green" meals. The fuelings are made up of over 60 items that are specifically low carbs but are high in probiotic cultures and Protein. The fuelings ultimately contain friendly bacteria that can help to boost gut health. They include cookies, bars, puddings, shakes, soups, cereals, and pasta.

Looking at the listed foods, you might think they are quite high in carbs, that is understandable, but the fuelings are composed in such a way that they are lower in sugar and carbs than the traditional versions of similar foods. The company does this by using small portion sizes and sugar substitutes. In furtherance to this, many of the fuelings are packed with soy protein isolate and whey protein powder. Those interested in the Optavia's diet plan but are not interested or got no chance to cook are provided with pre-made low-carb meals by the company.

What is the Optavia diet

The Optavia Diet is the brainchild of the man behind the multimillion-dollar company Medifast– Dr. William Vitale. Now carrying the brand Optavia since 2017, the goal of this diet is to encourage healthy and sustainable weight loss among its clientele. While there are many types of diet regimen that are available in the market, the Optavia Diet is ranked in the top 30 Best Diets in the United States.

Under this diet regimen, dieters are required to follow a weight plan that includes five feelings a day and one lean green meal daily. However, there are also other regimens of the Optavia Diet if the five fuelings a day is too much for you. And since this is a commercial diet, you have access to Optavia coaches and become part of a community that will encourage you to succeed in your weight loss journey. Moreover, this diet is also designed for people who want to transition from their old habits to healthier ones. Basically, this diet regimen is not only for people who want to lose weight but also for people who have diabetes, people suffering from gout, nursing moms, seniors as well as teens.

The Optavia Diet has been subjected to various studies to prove its efficacy in weight loss. Different studies were published in various journals indicating that those who follow this program are able to see significant changes in as little as 8 weeks and that people can achieve their long-term health goals with the Optavia Diet.

The Benefits of The Optavia Diet

It is easy to follow

The optavia diet plan is easy to follow as it relies on already prepared and packaged fuelings, and as such, you only have to cook 1-3 green and lean meals per day using the 5&1 diet plan. The plan comes along with sample meal logs and meal plans hence making it easy to follow.

It helps to improve blood pressure

The programs can also help improve patients' blood pressure through the loss of weight and low intake of sodium. Optavia meals are well made, such that they provide below 2,300mg of sodium per day, which is the recommended consumption level of sodium per day by the United States Department of Agriculture (USDA).

It helps to lose weight

The diet contributes/helps people who actively desire to lose weight and excess fat. It fixes this by reducing the number of calories and carbs taken in through its well-controlled portion meals and snacks. Studies have shown that a reduction in overall calorie intake can result in a more significant loss of weight; this is when full or partial meal replacement habits accompany it.

Coaches offer their support

Health coaches involved in optavia dieting are often available for consultation throughout the journey of losing weight or maintaining one's weight. And more research has shown that having access to a lifestyle coach can aid long-term weight maintenance as time goes on.

The Optavia Diet plans

The Optavia Diet encourages people to limit the number of calories that they should take daily. Under this program, dieters are encouraged to consume between 800 and 1000 calories daily. For this to be possible, dieters are encouraged to opt for healthier food items and meal replacements. But unlike other types of commercial diet regimens, the Optavia Diet comes in different variations. There are currently three variations of the Optavia Diet plan that one can choose according to one's needs.

5&1 Optavia Diet Plan: This is the most common version of the Optavia Diet, and it involves eating five prepackaged meals from the Optimal Health Fueling and one home-made balanced dinner.

4&2&1 Octavia Diet Plan: This diet plan is designed for people who want to have flexibility while following this regimen. Under this program, dieters are encouraged to eat more calories and have more flexible food choices. This means that they can consume four prepackaged Optimal Health Fueling food, three home-cooked meals from the Lean and Green, and one snack daily.

5&2&2 Optavia Diet Plan: This diet plan is perfect for individuals who prefer to have a flexible meal plan to achieve a healthy weight. It is recommended for a wide variety of people. Under this diet regimen, dieters must eat five fueling, two lean and green meals, and two healthy snacks.

3&3 Optavia Diet Plan: This particular Diet plan is created for people who have moderate weight problems and merely want to maintain a healthy body. Under this diet plan, dieters are encouraged to consume three prepackaged Optimal Health Fuelings and three home-cooked meals.

Optavia for Nursing Mothers: This diet regimen is designed for nursing mothers with babies of at least two months old. Aside from supporting breastfeeding mothers, it also encourages gradual weight loss.

Optavia for Diabetes: This Optavia Diet plan is designed for Type 1 and Type 2 diabetes people. The meal plans are designed to consume more green and lean meals, depending on their needs and condition.

Optavia for Gout: This diet regimen incorporates a balance of low in purines and moderate in protein.

Optavia for seniors (65 years and older): Designed for seniors, this Optavia Diet plan has some variations following the components of Fuelings depending on the senior dieters' needs and activities.

Optavia for Teen Boys and Optavia for Teen Girls (13-18 years old): Designed for active teens, the Optavia for Teens Boys and Optavia for Teens Girls provide the right nutrition to growing teens.

Regardless of which type of Optavia Diet plan you choose, you must talk with a coach to determine which program is right for you based on your individual goals. This is to ensure that you get the most out of the plan that you have chosen.

Food to eat and food to avoid

There are a lot many foods that you can eat while following the Optavia Diet. However, you must know these foods by heart. This is particularly true if you are just new to this diet, and you have to follow the 5&1 Optavia Diet Plan strictly. Thus, this section is dedicated to the types of foods that are recommended and those to avoid while following this diet regimen.

Foods to eat

There are numerous categories of foods that can be eaten under this diet regimen. This section will break down the Lean and Green foods that you can eat while following this diet regime.

Lean Foods

Leanest Foods - These foods are considered to be the leanest as it has only up to 4 grams of total fat. Moreover, dieters should eat a 7-ounce cooked portion of these foods. Consume these foods with 1 healthy fat serving.

☒ ☒ Fish: Flounder, cod, haddock, grouper, Mahi, tilapia, tuna (yellowfin fresh or canned), and wild catfish.

☒ ☒ Shellfish: Scallops, lobster, crabs, shrimp

☒ ☒ Game meat: Elk, deer, buffalo

☒ ☒ Ground turkey or other meat: Should be 98% lean

☒ ☒ Meatless alternatives: 14 egg whites, 2 cups egg substitute, 5 ounces seitan, 1 ½ cups 1% cottage cheese, and 12 ounces non-fat 0% Greek yogurt

Leaner Foods - These foods contain 5 to 9 grams of total fat. Consume these foods with 1 healthy fat serving. Make sure to consume only 6 ounces of a cooked portion of these foods daily:

☒ ☒ Fish: Halibut, trout, and swordfish

☒ ☒ Chicken: White meat such as breasts as long as the skin is removed

☒ ☒ Turkey: Ground turkey as long as it is 95% to 97% lean.

☒ ☒ Meatless options: 2 whole eggs plus 4 egg whites, 2 whole eggs plus one cup egg substitute, 1 ½ cups 2% cottage cheese, and 12 ounces low fat 2% plain Greek yogurt

Lean Foods - These are foods that contain 10g to 20g total fat. When consuming these foods, there should be no serving of healthy fat. These include the following:

☒ ☒ Fish: Tuna (bluefin steak), salmon, herring, farmed catfish, and mackerel

☒ ☒ Lean beef: Ground, steak, and roast

☒ ☒ Lamb: All cuts

☒ ☒ Pork: Pork chops, pork tenderloin, and all parts. Make sure to remove the skin

☒ ☒ Ground turkey and other meats: 85% to 94% lean

☒ ☒ Chicken: Any dark meat

☒ ☒ Meatless options: 15 ounces extra-firm tofu, 3 whole eggs (up to two times per week), 4 ounces reduced-fat skim cheese, 8 ounces part-skim ricotta cheese, and 5 ounces tempeh

Healthy Fat Servings - Healthy fat servings are allowed under this diet. They should contain 5 grams of fat and less than grams of carbohydrates. Regardless of what type of Optavia Diet plan you follow, make sure that you add between 0 and 2 healthy fat servings daily. Below are the different healthy fat servings that you can eat:

☒ ☒ 1 teaspoon oil (any kind of oil)

☒ ☒ 1 tablespoon low carbohydrate salad dressing

☒ ☒ 2 tablespoons reduced-fat salad dressing

☒ ☒ 5 to 10 black or green olives

☒ ☒ 1 ½ ounce avocado

☒ ☒ 1/3-ounce plain nuts including peanuts, almonds, pistachios

☒ ☒ 1 tablespoon plain seeds such as chia, sesame, flax, and pumpkin seeds

☒ ☒ ½ tablespoon regular butter, mayonnaise, and margarine

Green Foods

This section will discuss the green servings that you still need to consume while following the Optavia Diet Plan. These include all kinds of vegetables that have been categorized from lower, moderate, and high in terms of carbohydrate content. One serving of vegetables should be at ½ cup unless otherwise specified.

Lower Carbohydrate - These are vegetables that contain low amounts of carbohydrates. If you are following the 5&1 Optavia Diet plan, then these vegetables are good for you.

☒ ☒ A cup of green leafy vegetables, such as collard greens (raw), lettuce (green leaf, iceberg, butterhead, and romaine), spinach (raw), mustard greens, spring mix, bok choy (raw), and watercress.

☒ ☒ ½ cup of vegetables including cucumbers, celery, radishes, white mushroom, sprouts (mung bean, alfalfa), arugula, turnip greens, escarole, nopales, Swiss chard (raw), jalapeno, and bok choy (cooked).

Moderate Carbohydrate - These are vegetables that contain moderate amounts of carbohydrates. Below are the types of vegetables that can be consumed in moderation:

☒ ☒ ½ cup of any of the following vegetables such as asparagus, cauliflower, fennel bulb, eggplant, portabella mushrooms, kale, cooked spinach, summer squash (zucchini and scallop).

Higher Carbohydrates - Foods that are under this category contain a high amount of starch. Make sure to consume limited amounts of these vegetables.

⊠ ⊠ ½ cup of the following vegetables like chayote squash, red cabbage, broccoli, cooked collard and mustard greens, green or wax beans, kohlrabi, kabocha squash, cooked leeks, any peppers, okra, raw scallion, summer squash such as straightneck and crookneck, tomatoes, spaghetti squash, turnips, jicama, cooked Swiss chard, and hearts of palm.

Foods to avoid

The following foods are to be avoided, except it's included in the fuelings — they include:

•Fried foods: meats, fish, shellfish, vegetables, desserts like baked goods

•Refined grains: white bread, pasta, scones, hotcakes, flour tortillas, wafers, white rice, treats, cakes, cakes

•Certain fats: margarine, coconut oil, strong shortening

•Whole fat dairy: milk, cheddar, yogurt

•Alcohol: all varieties, no exception

•Sugar-sweetened beverages: pop, natural product juice, sports drinks, caffeinated drinks, sweet tea

The accompanying nourishments are beyond reach while on the 5&1 plan, however, included back during the 6-week progress stage and permitted during the 3&3 plan:

•Fruit: all kinds of fresh fruits

•Low fat or without fat dairy: yogurt, milk, cheddar

The Optavia diet is owned by Medifast and incorporates pre-bought, distributed dinners, as well as tidbits, low carb natively constructed suppers, and continuous training to support weight and fat misfortune.

The Optavia diet is claimed by Medifast, a feast substitution organization. The two fundamental diets, Medifast and Optavia, are low-calorie-carb-programs that join bundled nourishments with custom-made dinners to energize weight reduction.

In any case, dissimilar to Medifast, the Optavia diet remembers one-for-one instructing, and while you can look over a few choices, there's an all-incorporate-marked-item called "Optavia Fuelings", as well as custom-made entrées known as "Lean and Green" dinners.

Optavia Fueling involves more than 60 things that are low in carbs; however, they're high in protein and probiotic societies, which contain microscopic organisms that may help your guts wellbeing. These nourishments incorporate bars, treats, shakes, puddings, oats, soups, and pasta.

Even though they may appear to be very high in carbs, fuelings are intended to be lower in carbs and sugar than the conventional adaptations of similar nourishments. To achieve this, the organization utilizes sugar substitutes in bits.

For those not keen on cooking, the organization gives a line of pre-made-low-carb dinners called "Flavors of Home" that can supplant "Lean and Green" suppers.

The Optavia diet incorporates two health improvement plans and a weight support plan:

Optimal Weight 5&1 Plan

The most mainstream plan, this variant incorporates five Optavia "Fuelings" and one adjusted "Lean and Green" dinner every day.

Optimal Weight 4&2&1 Plan

For the individuals needing more calories or adaptability in food decisions, this arrangement incorporates 4 Optavia Fuelings, 2 "Lean and Green" dinners, and one nibble for every day.

Optimal Health 3&3 Plan

Intended for upkeep, this one incorporates three Optavia fuelings and three adjusted Lean and Green dinners every day.

The Optavia program gives extra instruments to help weight reduction and upkeep including tips and motivation employing instant messaging, network discussions, week-by-week bolster calls, and an application that permits you to set dinner updates and track food admission and movement.

Even though Optavia offers these particular plans, it's indistinct whether this diet is ok for individuals with certain ailments. Furthermore, young people and breastfeeding moms have an exceptional supplement and calorie needs that may not be met by the Optavia diet.

People with gout, diabetes, nursing mothers, teens, and seniors all have specific plans offered by the company that has been designed solely based on their conditions. Even though there are specialized programs for people with special medical conditions, you might need to talk to your doctor if you have an individual medical condition before going forth with the program. Nursing mothers and teenagers also have a specific calorie daily intake that may not be achieved if they follow the Optavia diet plan. Hence, it is best anyone in this category speak with his or her doctor before starting to avoid future health complications.

5&1 Optimal Weight

Consuming 6 small meals a day is the 1st Healthy Habit you will absorb. On the 5&1 Optimal Weight Plan, the body goes in a gentle but well-organized fat-burning state at the same time, maintaining and retaining lean

muscle mass. You can choose from more than sixty convenient, scientifically designed, and nutritionally inter-changeable fuelings including shakes, biscuits, soups, bars, pretzels, brownies, hot beverages, hearty choices and pudding. Each fueling has an approximately similar nutritional profile curated by our team of skilled food scientists and refined by our registered and expert dietitians and nutrition team.

In addition to consuming 5 fuelings per day, you will learn an alternative healthy habit, which is to know how to curate a "Lean & Green" food that is perfect for you and your loved ones. You will start to absorb what optimal nutrition appears to be and soon enough, healthy eating will be considered as second nature.

Our scientifically tested and proven 5&1 Optimal Weight Plan teaches the clients to consume 6 small meals a day, an essential practice that will help the clients sustain a healthy weight. It is easy to follow, fast, no-hassle and is based on the healthy habit of consuming 6 small meals per day, with an interval of one meal every 2-3 hours. With the support of your chosen Optavia Coach and our Community, you are guaranteed to start making progress instantly.

3&3 Optimal Health

This diet is intended for upkeep. It incorporates three Optavia fueling and three adjusted Lean and Green din-ners every day.

Once you have achieved your healthy weight, it is imperative to sustain the good habits you have learned, which includes fueling your body once every two to three hours. To aid in sustaining your healthy weight, we have developed the 3&3 Optimal Health Plan, which emphasizes on nutritionally well-adjusted small meals, consumed once every two to three hours (similar to that of the Optimal Weight 4&2&1 Plan), while incorporat-ing additional food choices in their right servings. Your chosen Optavia Coach can give more details regarding the 3&3 Optimal Health Plan developed by our team of registered and expert dietitians.

To be able to keep an eye on the 3 & 3 Optimal Health Plan, consume 3 Optimal Health Fuelings per day, with 3 balanced meals of your choice.

Which Optavia Diet plan is good for me?

As there are so many diet plans offered by Optavia, it is important to get in touch with a certified Optavia coach to learn about the many options that you have. It is crucial that you do not second-guess the diet plan that you are going to follow as each diet plan is designed to fit a particular profile. For instance, if you are a very active person, you can take on the Optavia 5&1 plan but then, the coach will also look at other factors such as your age

and health risks so that you can be matched with the right Optavia Diet Plan.

Chapter 3: Getting Started With Optavia

How to Start the Optavia Diet?

The Optavia Diet has two unique phases: Initial and Maintenance Phases. Upon enrollment, you will be assigned to a diet coach that will help you undertake all the necessary things to be a successful dieter. So, if you are wondering what steps you need to undertake while following the two phases, then this section will discuss just that.

The initial phase is when people are encouraged to limit their calorie intake from 800 to 1,000 calories for the next 12 weeks or until the dieter loses 12 pounds. For this phase, dieters are encouraged to consume "Lean and Green" meals, five to seven times daily. Moreover, dieters are also encouraged to consume 1 optional snack including sugar-free gelatin, celery sticks, and 12 ounces of nuts.

The maintenance phase, on the other hand, is implemented once you have already lost 12 pounds from your initial weight. During this phase, you can increase your calorie intake to 1,550 daily. This phase can last for 6 weeks. Moreover, you are also allowed to incorporate other foods such as whole grains, fruits, and low-fat dairy into your diet.

After the maintenance phase, you are now ready to follow your specific Optavia Diet plan. This is also the time when you need to consume not only "Lean and Green" meals but also fueling foods. The number of meals depends on the specific diet plan you choose. For instance, if you opt for the 3&3 Optavia plan, you need to consume three "Lean and Green" meals and three "Fuelings".

How to Follow the Optavia Diet?

While the Optavia Diet is all about delivering weight loss to its dieters, the success of dieters still largely depends on how they approach this particular diet regimen. Thus, if you want to become successful, below are the tips that you should do while following the Optavia Diet.

Opt for foods that are cooked using healthy cooking methods. Healthy cooking methods include baking, grilling, poaching, and broiling. Avoid frying your foods as cooking oil increases the calorie content of your food.

Portion sizes of your food should follow the Optavia recommendations. This means that the portion sizes refer to the cooked weight and not the raw weight of the ingredients that you are using.

Opt for foods that are rich in Omega-3 fatty acids such as tuna, salmon, mackerel, trout, herring, and many other cold-water fishes. Omega-3 fatty acids contribute to lowering inflammation in the body.

Choose meatless alternatives such as tofu and tempeh. They are rich in proteins but not too much on calories.

Following the program at all costs even if you are dining out. This means that you have to consume healthy meals when you eat out and make sure that you stay away from alcohol.

To follow the diet first off, you must start with a conversation with the Optavia diet coach to determine which Optavia plan is best suited for your goal. It could be weight loss or weight maintenance, and make yourself familiar with the Plan.

Initial Steps

Most people begin with the Optimum Weight 5&1 Diet for weight reduction, an 800 to 1,000 calorie routine that will help you lose 12 pounds over 12 weeks. You are expected to consume one meal every 2-3 hours and have moderate activity for half an hour on some days of the week. In general, no more than 100 grams of carbs are given per day by the Fuelings and portions. As Optavia coaches get paid on commission, you will order these meals from your coach's specific page.

Lean and Green meals aim to be high in protein and low in carbs. One meal provides 5, 7(cooked) ounces of lean protein, 3 portions of vegetables mostly non-starchy, and up to 2 portions of good fats. This schedule also involves one extra snack a day (which the coach would accept), 3 celery sticks, half a cup of sugar-free gelatin, or a half-ounce of nuts are plan-approved treats. Bear in mind that the 5&1 Strategy does not allow alcohol intake.

Maintenance Phase

When you achieve the target weight, you begin a six-week maintenance period, which entails steadily raising calories to 1,550 calories but not more than that each day and incorporating low-fat dairy, whole grains, and fruits in a larger range of foods.

You are expected to switch over to the "Ideal Wellness" 3&3 Schedule after six weeks, which involves 3 "Lean & Green" meals and 3 Fuels every day with regular Optavia coaching. Many who have had continuous progress on the platform have the possibility of being qualified as a coach for Optavia.

Below is the breakdown comparison of meals' nutritional content on the Optavial Weight 5&1 Plan and the federal government's 2015 Dietary Guidelines for Americans.

Optimal Weight 5&1 Plan

Federal Government Recommer

Calories

800-1,000

Men

19-25: 2,800

26-45: 2,600

46-65: 2,400

65+: 2,200

Women

19-25: 2,200

26-50: 2,000

51+: 1,800

Total fat

% of Calorie Intake

20%

20%-35%

Total Carbohydrates

% of Calorie Intake

40%

45%-65%

Sugars

10%-20%

N/A

Fiber

25 g – 30 g

Men

19-30: 34 g.

31-50: 31 g.

51+: 28 g.

Women

19-30: 28 g.

31-50: 25 g.

51+: 22 g.

Protein

40%

10%-35%

Sodium

Under 2,300 mg

Under 2,300 mg.

Potassium

Average 3,000 mg

At least 4,700 mg.

Calcium

1,000 mg – 1,200 mg

Men

1,000 mg.

Women

19-50: 1,000 mg.

51+: 1,200 mg.

eos dolume re, sit a natur?

Blackened Salmon with Avocado Salsa

Prep Time	Cook Time	Serving
30 Minutes	21 Minutes	6

Ingredients

1 tablespoon. extra virgin olive oil

4 filets of salmon (about 6 ozs. each)

4 teaspoons. Cajun seasoning

2 med. avocados, diced

1 cup cucumber, diced

¼ cup red onion, diced

1 tablespoon. parsley, chopped

1 tablespoon. lime juice

Sea salt & pepper, to taste

Directions

1. Heat a skillet over medium-high heat and warm the oil in it.

2. Rub the Cajun seasoning into the fillets, then lay them into the bottom of the skillet once it's hot enough.

3. Cook until a dark crust forms, then flip and repeat.

4. In a medium mixing bowl, combine all the ingredients for the salsa and set aside.

5. Plate the fillets and top with ¼ of the salsa yielded.

6. Enjoy!

Nutrition:

Calories: 445 Cal

Fat: 31 g

Carbs: 6 g

Protein: 10 g

Fiber: 5 g

Delectable Tomato Slices

Prep Time	Cook Time	Serving
15 Minutes	15 Minutes	10

Ingredients

½ cup of. mayonnaise

½ cup of. ricotta cheese, shredded

½ cup part-skim mozzarella cheese, shredded

½ cup of parmesan and Romano cheese blend, grated

1 teaspoon. garlic, minced

1 tablespoon. dried oregano, crushed

Salt, to taste

4 large tomatoes, cut each one in 5 slices

Directions

1. Preheat the oven to broiler on high. Arrange a rack about 3-inch from the heating element.

2. In a bowl, add the mayonnaise, cheeses, garlic, oregano, and salt and mix until well combined and smooth.

3. Spread the cheese mixture over each tomato slice evenly.

4. Arrange the tomato slices onto a broiler pan in a single layer.

5. Broil for about 3-5 minutes or until the top becomes golden brown.

6. Remove from the oven and transfer the tomato slices onto a platter.

7. Set aside to cool slightly.

8. Serve warm.

Nutrition:

Calories: 110 Cal

Fat: 29 g

Carbs: 2 g

Protein: 16 g

Fiber: 5 g

Air Fryer Buffalo Cauliflower

Ingredients

Homemade buffalo sauce: 1/2 cup
One head of cauliflower, cut bite-size pieces
Butter melted: 1 tablespoon
Olive oil
Kosher salt & pepper, to taste

Prep Time	Cook Time	Serving
-	15 Minutes	4

Nutrition:

Calories 101kcal | Carbohydrates 4g | Protein 3g | Fat: 7g

Directions

1. Spray cooking oil on the air fryer basket.

2. In a bowl, add buffalo sauce, melted butter, pepper, and salt. Mix well.

3. Put the cauliflower bits in the air fryer and spray the olive oil over it. Let it cook at 400 F for 7 minutes.

4. Remove the cauliflower from the air fryer and add it to the sauce. Coat the cauliflower well.

5. Put the sauce coated cauliflower back into the air fryer.

6. Cook at 400 F, for 7-8 minutes or until crispy.

7. Take out from the air fryer and serve with leaner protein.

Low Carb Air-fried Calzones

Ingredients

Cooked chicken breast: 1/3 cup(shredded)
One teaspoon olive oil
Spinach leaves(baby): 3 cups
Whole-wheat pizza dough, freshly prepared
Marinara sauce: 1/3 cup(lower-sodium)
Diced red onion:1/4 cup
Skim mozzarella cheese: 6 Tbsp.
Cooking spray

Prep Time	Cook Time	Serving
-	27 minutes	2

Nutrition:

Calories 348|Fat 12g | Protein 21g |Carbohydrate 18g

Directions

1. In a medium skillet, over a medium flame, add oil, onions. Sauté until soft. Then add spinach leaves, cook until wilted. Turn off the heat and add chicken and marinara sauce.

2. Cut the dough into two pieces.

3. Add 1/4 of the spinach mix on each circle dough piece.

4. Add skim shredded cheese on top. Fold the dough over and crimp the edges.

5. Spray the calzones with cooking spray.

6. Put calzones in the air fryer. Cook for 12 minutes, at 325°F until dough is light brown. Turn the calzone over and cook for eight more minutes.

Tasty Kale & Celery Crackers

Ingredients

One cups flax seed, ground
1 cups flax seed, soaked overnight and drained
2 bunches kale, chopped
1 bunch basil, chopped
½ bunch celery, chopped
2 garlic cloves, minced
1/3 cup olive oil

Prep Time	Cook Time	Serving
-	20 minutes	6

Nutrition:

calories 143|fat 1g| fiber 2g| carbs 8g| Protein 4g

Directions

1. Mix the ground flaxseed with the celery, kale, basil, and garlic in your food processor and mix well.

2. Add the oil and soaked flaxseed, then mix again, scatter in the pan of your air fryer, break into medium crackers and cook for 20 minutes at 380 degrees F.

3. Serve as an appetizer and break into cups.

4. Enjoy

Sweet Chipotle Grilled Beef Ribs

Ingredients

4 tbsp sugar-free BBQ sauce + extra for serving
2 tbsp erythritol
Pink salt and black pepper to taste
2 tbsp olive oil
2 tsp chipotle powder
1 tsp garlic powder
1 lb beef spare ribs

Prep Time	Cook Time	Serving
10 Minutes	35 Minutes	4

Directions

1. Mix the erythritol, salt, pepper, oil, chipotle, and garlic powder. Brush on the meaty sides of the ribs and wrap in foil. Sit for 30 minutes to marinate.

2. Preheat oven to 400°F. Place wrapped ribs on a baking sheet and cook for 40 minutes until cooked through. Remove ribs and aluminium foil, brush with BBQ sauce, and brown under the broiler for 10 minutes on both sides. Slice and serve with extra BBQ sauce and lettuce tomato salad.

Nutrition:

Kcal 395
Fat 33g
Net Carbs 3g
Protein 21g

Grilled Sirloin Steak with Sauce Diane

Ingredients

Sirloin steak
1 ½ lb sirloin steak
Salt and black pepper to taste
1 tsp olive oil
Sauce Diane
1 tbsp olive oil
1 clove garlic, minced
1 cup sliced porcini mushrooms
1 small onion, finely diced
2 tbsp butter
1 tbsp Dijon mustard
2 tbsp Worcestershire sauce
¼ cup whiskey
2 cups heavy cream

Prep Time	Cook Time	Serving
10 Minutes	25 Minutes	6

Directions

1. Put a grill pan over high heat and as it heats, brush the steak with oil, sprinkle with salt and pepper, and rub the seasoning into the meat with your hands. Cook the steak in the pan for 4 minutes on each side for medium-rare and transfer to a chopping board to rest for 4 minutes before slicing. Reserve the juice.

2. Heat the oil in a frying pan over medium heat and sauté the onion for 3 minutes. Add the butter, garlic, and mushrooms, and cook for 2 minutes. Add the Worcestershire sauce, the reserved juice, and mustard.

3. Stir and cook for 1 minute. Pour in the whiskey and cook further 1 minute until the sauce reduces by half. Swirl the pan and add the cream. Let it simmer to thicken for about 3 minutes. Adjust the taste with salt and pepper. Spoon the sauce over the steaks slices and serve with celeriac mash.

Nutrition:

Kcal 434
Fat 17g
Net Carbs 2.9g
Protein 36g

Easy Zucchini Beef Lasagna

Ingredients

1 lb ground beef
2 large zucchinis, sliced lengthwise
3 cloves garlic
1 medium white onion, chopped
3 tomatoes, chopped
Salt and black pepper to taste
2 tsp sweet paprika
1 tsp dried thyme
1 tsp dried basil
1 cup mozzarella cheese, shredded
1 tbsp olive oil

Prep Time	Cook Time	Serving
25 Minutes	1 hour	4

Directions

1. Preheat the oven to 370°F. Heat the olive oil in a skillet over medium heat. Cook the beef for 4 minutes while breaking any lumps as you stir. Top with onion, garlic, tomatoes, salt, paprika, and pepper. Stir and continue cooking for 5 minutes. Lay 1/3 of the zucchini slices in the baking dish.

2. Top with 1/3 of the beef mixture and repeat the layering process two more times with the same quantities. Season with basil and thyme. Sprinkle the mozzarella cheese on top and tuck the baking dish in the oven. Bake for 35 minutes. Remove the lasagna and let it rest for 10 minutes before serving.

Nutrition:

Kcal 344
Fat 17.8g
Net Carbs 2.9g
Protein 40.4g

Snacks

Chicken Parmesan

Prep Time	Cook Time	Serving
20 Minutes	15 Minutes	4

Ingredients

¼ cup of avocado oil

¼ cup of almond flour

¼ cup parmesan cheese, grated

¾ cup of marinara sauce, sugar-free

¾ cup mozzarella cheese, shredded

2 eggs, beaten

2 teaspoons. Italian seasoning

3 oz. pork rinds, pulverized

4 lbs. chicken breasts, boneless & skinless

Sea salt & pepper, to taste

Nutrition:

Calories: 621 Cal

Fat: 24 g

Carbs: 6 g

Protein: 14 g

Fiber: 6 g

Directions

1. Preheat the oven to 450° Fahrenheit and grease a baking dish.

2. Place the beaten egg into one shallow dish. Place the almond flour in another. In a third dish, combine the pork rinds, parmesan, and Italian seasoning and mix well.

3. Pat the chicken breasts dry and pound them down to about ½" thick.

4. Dredge the chicken in the almond flour, then coat in egg, then coat in crumb.

5. Heat a large sauté pan over medium-high heat and warm oil until shimmering.

6. Once the oil is hot, lay the breasts into the pan and do not move them until they've had a chance to cook. Cook for about two minutes, then flip as gently as possible (a fish spatula is perfect) then cook for two more. Remove the pan from the heat.

7. Place the breasts in the greased baking dish and top with marinara sauce and mozzarella cheese.

8. Bake for about 10 minutes.

9. Serve!

Breakfast Recipes

Eggplant Breakfast Spread

Prep Time	Cook Time	Serving
5 Minutes	10 Minutes	6

Ingredients

4 tablespoons olive oil
2 pounds eggplants, peeled and roughly chopped
4 garlic cloves, minced
A pinch of salt and black pepper
1 cup water
¼ cup lemon juice
1 tablespoon sesame seeds paste
¼ cup black olives, pitted
A few sprigs thyme, chopped
A drizzle of olive oil

Directions

1. Set your instant pot on sauté mode, add oil, heat it up, add eggplant pieces, stir and sauté for 5 minutes

2. Add garlic, salt, pepper and the water, stir gently, cover and cook on High for 5 minutes.

3. Discard excess water, add sesame seeds paste, lemon juice and olives and blend using an immersion blender.

4. Transfer to a bowl, sprinkle chopped thyme, drizzle some oil and serve for a fancy breakfast.

Enjoy!

Nutrition: *calories 163, fat 2, fiber 1, carbs 5, protein 7*

Hasbrown Casserole

Ingredients

48 ounces hashbrowns
6 eggs, whisked
1 yellow onion, chopped
¼ cup milk
3 tablespoons olive oil
½ cup cheddar cheese, shredded
1 pound ham, chopped

Prep Time	Cook Time	Serving
10 Minutes	30 Minutes	10

Nutrition:

calories 261, fat 14, fiber 1, carbs 20, protein 14

Directions

1. Set your Foodi on sauté mode, add the oil, heat it up, add the onion, stir and cook for 3-4 minutes.

2. Add hashbrowns and the ham, set the Foodi on Air Crisp and cook for 15 minutes, stirring everything halfway.

3. Add eggs mixed with hashbrowns, and cook everything on Air Crisp for 10 minutes more.

4. Sprinkle the cheese on top, divide everything between plates and serve for breakfast.

Mushroom Spread

Ingredients

1 ounce porcini mushrooms, dried
1 pound button mushrooms, sliced
1 cup hot water
1 tablespoon ghee
1 tablespoon olive oil
1 shallot, chopped
¼ cup cold water
A pinch of salt and pepper
1 bay leaf

Prep Time	Cook Time	Serving
10 minutes	14 minutes	6

Nutrition:

calories 152, fat 4, fiber 2, carbs 5, protein 7

Directions

1. Put porcini mushrooms in a bowl, add 1 cup hot water and leave aside for now.

2. Set your instant pot on Sauté mode, add ghee and oil and heat it up.

3. Add shallot, stir and sauté for 2 minutes

4. Add porcini mushrooms and their liquid, fresh mushrooms, cold, salt, pepper and bay leaf, stir, cover and cook on High for 12 minutes,

5. Discard bay leaf and some of the liquid and blend mushrooms mix using an immersion blender.

6. Transfer to small bowls and serve as a breakfast spread.

Enjoy!

Breakfast Chia Pudding

Ingredients

½ cup chia seeds
2 cups almond milk
¼ cup almonds
¼ cup coconut, shredded
4 teaspoons sugar

Prep Time	Cook Time	Serving
2 hours	3 minutes	4

Nutrition:

calories 130, fat 1, fiber 4, carbs 2, protein 14

Directions

1. Put chia seeds in your instant pot.

2. Add milk, almonds and coconut flakes, stir, cover and cook at High for 3 minutes.

3. Release the pressure quick, divide the pudding between bowls, top each with a teaspoon of sugar and serve.

Enjoy!

Breakfast Sweet Potatoes

Prep Time	Cook Time	Serving
5 Minutes	7 Minutes	2

Ingredients

4 sweet potatoes
2 teaspoons Italian seasoning
1 tablespoon bacon fat
1 cup chives, chopped for serving.
Water
Salt and pepper to the taste

Directions

1. Put potatoes in your instant pot, add water to cover them, cover the pot and cook at High for 10 minutes.

2. Release the pressure naturally, transfer potatoes to a working surface and leave them to cool down.

3. Peel potatoes, transfer them to a bowl and mash them a bit with a fork.

4. Set your instant pot on sauté mode, add bacon fat and heat up.

5. Add potatoes, seasoning, salt and pepper to the taste, stir, cover the pot and cook at High for 1 minute.

6. Release the pressure quickly, stir potatoes again, divide them between plates and serve with chives sprinkled on top.

Enjoy!

Nutrition: calories 90, fat 3, fiber 1, carbs 6, protein 7

Delicious Korean Eggs

Ingredients

1 and 1/3 cup water
1 egg
A pinch of garlic powder
A pinch of sea salt and black pepper
A pinch of sesame seeds
1 teaspoon scallions, chopped

Prep Time	Cook Time	Serving
10 Minutes	5 Minutes	1

Nutrition:

calories 100, fat 1, fiber 2, carbs 2, protein 4

Directions

1. Crack the egg into a bowl, add 1/3 cup water and whisk well.

2. Strain this into a heat proof bowl, add garlic powder, salt, pepper, scallions and sesame seeds and whisk again.

3. Put 1 cup water in your instant pot, add the steamer basket and place the bowl with the egg mixture inside.

4. Cover, cook on High for 5 minutes.

5. Transfer to a plate and serve.

Enjoy!

Great French Eggs

Ingredients

1 yellow onion, chopped
6 eggs
1 cup bacon, cooked and crumbled
1 cup kale, chopped
1 teaspoon herbs de Provence
1 cup water
A pinch of sea salt and black pepper

Prep Time	Cook Time	Serving
10 minutes	20 minutes	6

Nutrition:

calories 132, fat 3, fiber 1, carbs 4, protein 7

Directions

1. In a bowl, mix eggs with onion, kale, bacon, salt, pepper and herbs, whisk really well and pour into a heat proof dish.

2. Put the water in your instant pot, add the steamer basket and put the dish with the eggs inside.

3. Cover, cook on High for 20 minutes, leave aside to cool down a bit, divide among plates and serve.

Enjoy!

Different Eggs Breakfast

Ingredients

2 tablespoons olive oil
1 cup water
1 cup sweet potatoes, cubed
2 eggs
1 jalapeno pepper, chopped
½ cup yellow onion, chopped
1 tablespoon cilantro, chopped
A pinch of salt and black pepper

Prep Time	Cook Time	Serving
10 minutes	10 minutes	2

Nutrition:

calories 142, fat 2, fiber 1, carbs 3, protein 6

Directions

1. Put 1 cup water in your instant pot, add the steamer basket, place cubed potatoes inside, cover, cook on High for 3 minutes and transfer to a bowl.

2. Take the steamer basket out, clean instant pot, add the oil and set the pot on Sauté mode.

3. Add onion, jalapeno and return potato cubes, stir and sauté for a couple of minutes.

4. Crack eggs, season with a pinch of salt, black pepper and sprinkle cilantro.

5. Stir gently, cover and cook on High for 2 minutes.

6. Divide this breakfast mix between plates and serve.

Enjoy!

Delicious Breakfast Casserole

Prep Time	Cook Time	Serving
10 Minutes	30 Minutes	6

Ingredients

1 and 1/3 cups leek, chopped
2 tablespoons coconut oil
2 teaspoons garlic, minced
8 eggs
1 cup kale, chopped
2/3 cup sweet potato, grated
1 and ½ cups sausage, cooked and sliced
1 and ½ cups water

Directions

1. Set your instant pot on sauté mode, add oil and heat it up.

2. Add kale, leeks and garlic, stir, cook for 3 minutes, transfer to a bowl and clean the pot.

3. Meanwhile, in a bowl, mix eggs with sausage, sautéed veggies and sweet potato, whisk really well and pour into a heat proof dish.

4. Add the water to your instant pot, add the steamer basket, place the dish with the eggs mix inside, cover and cook on Manual for 25 minutes.

5. Divide among plates and serve for breakfast.

Nutrition: *calories 254, fat 4, fiber 1, carbs 4, protein 20*

Hearty Breakfast

Prep Time	Cook Time	Serving
10 Minutes	20 Minutes	6

Ingredients

3 pounds pork roast, boneless
2 teaspoons cumin, ground
1 teaspoon red pepper flakes, crushed
A pinch of sea salt and black pepper
1 teaspoon oregano, dried
Juice from 1 orange
Orange peel from 1 orange, grated
6 garlic cloves, minced
1 yellow onion, chopped
1 bay leaf
1 tablespoon avocado oil
2 teaspoons cilantro, chopped
1 butter lettuce head, torn
2 radishes, sliced
2 avocados, pitted, peeled and sliced
1 cup Paleo salsa
2 jalapenos, chopped
3 limes, quartered

Directions

1. Put roast in your instant pot.

2. Add cumin, pepper flakes, salt, pepper, oregano, orange juice, orange peel, garlic, yellow onion, bay leaf and oil and rub roast well.

3. Cover instant pot and cook on High for 20 minutes.

4. Transfer roast to a cutting board, leave aside to cool down a bit, shred and divide among plates.

5. Also divide lettuce leaves, radishes, avocado slices, jalapenos and lime wedges.

6. Sprinkle cilantro, divide salsa on top and serve for breakfast.

Enjoy!

Nutrition:

calories 275, fat 4, fiber 1, carbs 5, protein 14

Great Egg Casserole

Prep Time	Cook Time	Serving
10 Minutes	3 hours	6

Ingredients

32 ounces sweet potatoes, cubed
1 cup coconut milk
2 cups ham, chopped
1 yellow onion, chopped
12 eggs
A pinch of salt and black pepper
Cooking spray

Directions

1. In a bowl, mix eggs with salt, pepper, onion, ham, sweet potatoes and milk and whisk well.

2. Spray your instant pot with some cooking spray, add eggs mix, cover and cook on Low for 3 hours.

3. Divide among plates and serve hot.

Enjoy!

Nutrition:

calories 275, fat 4, fiber 1, carbs 5, protein 14

Breakfast Quiche

Prep Time	Cook Time	Serving
10 Minutes	30 Minutes	6

Ingredients

1 cup water

6 eggs, whisked

A pinch of black pepper

½ cup coconut milk

4 bacon slices, cooked and crumbled

1 cup sausage, cooked and ground

½ cup ham, chopped

2 green onions, choppe

Directions

1. Put the water in your instant pot and add the steamer basket inside.

2. Put bacon, sausage and ham in a bowl, mix and spread on the bottom of a quiche dish.

3. In a bowl, mix eggs with black pepper, coconut milk and green onions and whisk well.

4. Pour this over meat, spread, place inside the pot, cover and cook on High for 30 minutes.

5. Slice, divide among plates and serve.

Enjoy!

Nutrition: *calories 243, fat 3, fiber 1, carbs 6, protein 12*

Wonderful Frittata

Prep Time	Cook Time	Serving
10 Minutes	18 Minutes	4

Ingredients

4 ounces sweet potatoes, cut into medium fries
6 eggs
A pinch of sea salt and black pepper
1 tablespoon olive oil
¼ cup scallions, chopped
1 garlic clove, minced
¼ cup coconut milk
1 teaspoon Paleo tomato paste
1 and ½ cups water
1 green bell pepper, chopped

Directions

1. Grease a heat proof dish with the oil and spread sweet potato fries on the bottom.

2. In a bowl, mix eggs with salt, pepper, scallions, garlic and bell pepper and whisk well.

3. In another bowl, mix coconut milk with tomato paste and stir.

4. Pour this over eggs mix, stir well and spread everything on top of sweet potato fries.

5. Put the water in your instant pot, add the steamer basket inside and place the eggs mix in the basket.

6. Cover, cook on High for 18 minutes, slice, divide among plates and serve hot.

Nutrition:

calories 153, fat 7, fiber 2, carbs 5, protein 15

Pumpkin and Apple Butter

Prep Time	Cook Time	Serving
10 Minutes	10 minutes	8

Ingredients

3 apples, peeled, cored and chopped
30 ounces pumpkin puree
1 tablespoon pumpkin pie spice
1 cup honey
12 ounces apple cider

Directions

1. Put pumpkin puree in your instant pot.

2. Add apples, pumpkin pie spice, cider and honey, stir well, cover and cook on High for 10 minutes.

3. Divide into jars, seal them and serve for breakfast whenever you want.

Enjoy!

Nutrition:

calories 100, fat 3, fiber 1, carbs 4, protein 6

Breakfast Spinach Delight

Prep Time	Cook Time	Serving
10 Minutes	20 Minutes	4

Ingredients

1 pound mustard leaves
1 pound spinach, torn
2 tablespoons olive oil
A small ginger piece, grated
2 yellow onions, chopped
4 garlic cloves, minced
1 teaspoon cumin, ground
1 teaspoon coriander, ground
1 teaspoon garam masala
A pinch of cayenne pepper
½ teaspoon turmeric
A pinch of black pepper
A pinch of fenugreek leaves, dried

Directions

1. Set your instant pot on Sauté mode, add oil and heat it up.

2. Add onion, garlic, ginger, coriander, cumin, garam masala, turmeric, cayenne pepper, black pepper and fenugreek, stir and cook for 5 minutes.

3. Add spinach and mustard leaves, stir gently, cover and cook on High for 15 minutes.

4. Divide into bowls and serve for breakfast.

Enjoy!

Nutrition: *calories 200, fat 3, fiber 2, carbs 5, protein 7*

Delicious Breakfast Cobbler

Prep Time	Cook Time	Serving
10 Minutes	10 Minutes	4

Ingredients

1 apple, cored and chopped
1 pear, chopped
2 tablespoons honey
1 plum, chopped
½ teaspoon cinnamon, ground
3 tablespoons coconut oil
¼ cup coconut, unsweetened and shredded
2 tablespoons sunflower seeds
2 tablespoons pecans, chopped

Directions

1. Put the oil in your instant pot and heat it up on Sauté mode.

2. Add the apple, pear, plum and honey in your instant pot, stir, cover and cook on Steam mode for 10 minutes.

3. Divide among plates, sprinkle sunflower seeds, pecans, coconut, and serve.

Enjoy!

Nutrition:

calories 154, fat 2, fiber 2, carbs 5, protein 3

Amazing Bacon And Sweet Potato Breakfast

Prep Time	Cook Time	Serving
10 Minutes	10 minutes	4

Ingredients

2 pounds sweet potatoes, cubed
A pinch of salt and black pepper
3 bacon strips
2 tablespoons water
2 teaspoons parsley, dried
1 teaspoon garlic powder
4 eggs, fried for serving

Directions

1. In your instant pot, mix sweet potatoes with bacon, salt, pepper, water, parsley and garlic powder, stir, cover and cook on High for 10 minutes.

2. Divide among plates next to fried eggs and serve.

Enjoy!

Nutrition:

calories 200, fat 2, fiber 2, carbs 6, protein 8

Great Veggie Quiche

Prep Time	Cook Time	Serving
10 Minutes	30 Minutes	8

Ingredients

½ cup almond milk

½ cup almond flour

8 eggs

A pinch of sea salt and black pepper

1 red bell pepper, chopped

2 green onions, chopped

1 cup tomatoes, chopped

½ cup zucchinis, chopped

1 cup water

Directions

1. In a bowl, mix eggs with almond flour, almond milk, salt, pepper, red bell pepper, green onions, zucchinis and tomatoes, whisk well, pour this into a round baking dish.

2. Put the water in your instant pot, add the steamer basket, add the baking dish inside, cover and cook on High for 30 minutes.

3. Leave quiche to cool down a bit, slice, divide among plates and serve.

Enjoy!

Nutrition: *calories 200, fat 3, fiber 2, carbs 5, protein 7*

Tomato And Spinach Breakfast Mix

Prep Time	Cook Time	Serving
10 Minutes	20 Minutes	6

Ingredients

12 eggs
A pinch of salt and black pepper
½ cup coconut milk
3 cups baby spinach, chopped
1 cup tomato, chopped
1 and ½ cups water
3 green onions, chopped

Directions

1. In a bowl, mix eggs with salt, pepper, milk, spinach, tomato and green onions and whisk well.

2. Pour this into a round baking dish.

3. Put the water in your instant pot, add the steamer basket, place the dish inside, cover and cook on High for 20 minutes.

4. Divide among plates and serve for breakfast.

Enjoy!

Nutrition:

calories 210, fat 3, fiber 3, carbs 4, protein 4

Special Breakfast Egg Muffins

Prep Time	Cook Time	Serving
10 Minutes	10 minutes	4

Ingredients

1 green onion, chopped
4 eggs
¼ teaspoon lemon pepper
4 bacon slices, cooked and crumbled
1 and ½ cups water

Directions

1. In a bowl, mix eggs with green onion, bacon and lemon pepper, whisk well and divide this into 4 muffin cups.

2. Put the water in your instant pot, add the steamer basket, place muffin cups inside, cover and cook on High for 8 minutes.

3. Divide egg muffins between plates and serve.

Enjoy!

Nutrition:

calories 172, fat 4, fiber 2, carbs 6, protein 7

Breakfast Scotch Eggs

Prep Time	Cook Time	Serving
10 Minutes	12 Minutes	4

Ingredients

1 pound sausage, ground
4 eggs
1 tablespoon olive oil
2 cups water

Directions

1. Put 1 cup water in your instant pot, add the steamer basket and put the eggs inside.

2. Cover, cook on High for 6 minutes, transfer eggs to a cutting board, cool them down and peel.

3. Divide sausage mix into 4 pieces, flatten each, add an egg in the center of each and wrap well.

4. Put the oil in your instant pot and set it on Sauté mode.

5. Add scotch eggs, brown them on all sides and transfer to a plate.

6. Add 1 cup water to the pot, add the steamer basket, add scotch eggs, cover and cook on High for 6 minutes.

7. Divide eggs between plates and serve.

Enjoy!

Nutrition: *calories 210, fat 3, fiber 5, carbs 6, protein 6*

Wonderful Breakfast Omelet

Prep Time	Cook Time	Serving
10 Minutes	30 Minutes	6

Ingredients

1 and ½ cups water
4 spring onions, chopped
6 ounces bacon, chopped
½ cup red, green and orange bell peppers, chopped
A pinch of black pepper
6 eggs
½ cup coconut milk
Olive oil spray

Directions

1. In a bowl, mix eggs with a pinch of black pepper and coconut milk and whisk well.

2. Add mixed bell peppers, bacon and spring onions and whisk again.

3. Spray a round dish with olive oil spray, pour eggs mix and spread.

4. Put the water in your instant pot, add the steamer basket and the baking dish inside, cover and cook on High for 30 minutes.

5. Leave your omelet to cool down a bit, slice, divide among plates and serve.

Enjoy!

Nutrition:

calories 182, fat 2, fiber 2, carbs 6, protein 12

Superb Zucchini Breakfast

Prep Time	Cook Time	Serving
10 Minutes	5 minutes	6

Ingredients

1 and ½ cups yellow onion, chopped
1 tablespoon olive oil
2 garlic cloves, minced
12 ounces mushrooms, chopped
1 basil spring, chopped
A pinch of sea salt and black pepper
8 cups zucchinis, sliced
15 ounces canned tomatoes, crushed

Directions

1. Put the oil in your instant pot and heat it up on Sauté mode.

2. Add onion and garlic, stir and cook for 2 minutes.

3. Add mushrooms, basil, salt and pepper, stir and cook for 1 minute more.

4. Add zucchinis and tomatoes, stir, cover and cook on High for 2 minutes.

5. Divide among plates and serve for breakfast.

Enjoy!

Nutrition:

calories 176, fat 2, fiber 3, carbs 5, protein 6

Poached Eggs

Prep Time	Cook Time	Serving
10 Minutes	2 Minutes	3

Ingredients

A drizzle of olive oil
3 tablespoons coconut cream
1 tablespoons chives, chopped
3 eggs
1 cup water
A pinch of sea salt and black pepper

Directions

1. Grease 3 ramekins with some olive oil and divide coconut cream in each.

2. Crack an egg into each ramekin, season with a pinch of salt and pepper and sprinkle chives all over.

3. Put the water in your instant pot, add the steamer basket and place all 3 ramekins inside.

4. Cover instant pot and cook on High for 2 minutes.

5. Divide poached eggs between plates and serve.

Enjoy!

Nutrition: *calories 200, fat 2, fiber 1, carbs 2, protein 6*

Delicious Breakfast Eggs And Sauce

Prep Time	Cook Time	Serving
10 Minutes	12 Minutes	4

Ingredients

2 garlic cloves, minced
1 tablespoon coconut oil
1 red bell pepper, chopped
1 small yellow onion, chopped
1 teaspoon chili powder
½ teaspoon cumin, ground
½ teaspoon paprika
A pinch of salt and black pepper
1 and ½ cups Paleo and sugar free marinara sauce
A handful parsley, chopped
4 eggs

Directions

1. Set your instant pot on Sauté mode, add the oil and heat it up.

2. Add onion, bell pepper, garlic, paprika, cumin and chili powder, stir and sauté for 5 minutes.

3. Add sauce, stir and cook for 1 minute more.

4. Crack eggs into the sauce, cover the pot and cook on Low for 1 minute.

5. Season with a pinch of salt and black pepper, sprinkle parsley, divide among plates and serve.

Enjoy!

Nutrition:

calories 200, fat 2, fiber 1, carbs 3, protein 7

Light Breakfast

Prep Time	Cook Time	Serving
10 Minutes	10 minutes	4

Ingredients

1 tablespoon olive oil
2 yellow onions, chopped
6 zucchinis, chopped
1 pound cherry tomatoes, halved
1 cup water
2 garlic cloves, minced
A pinch of sea salt and black pepper
1 bunch basil, chopped

Directions

1. Set your instant pot on Sauté mode, add the oil and heat it up.

2. Add onions, tomatoes, water, zucchini, garlic, salt and pepper, stir, cover and cook on High for 5 minutes.

3. Sprinkle basil, toss gently, divide among plates and serve for breakfast.

Enjoy!

Nutrition:

calories 120, fat 2, fiber 1, carbs 3, protein 6

Great Zucchini Spread

Prep Time	Cook Time	Serving
20 Minutes	8 Minutes	4

Ingredients

2 tablespoons olive oil
3 pounds zucchinis, peeled and roughly chopped
3 garlic cloves, minced
2 yellow onions, chopped
2 carrots, chopped
½ cup water
1/3 cup tomatoes, crushed
2 bay leaves
A pinch of cayenne pepper
A pinch of salt and black pepper

Directions

1. Put zucchinis in a bowl, add some salt, toss, leave aside for 20 minutes and drain excess water.

2. Put the oil in your instant pot, set on sauté mode and heat it up.

3. Add carrots, zucchinis and onions, stir and sauté for 5 minutes.

4. Add bay leaves, a pinch of salt, pepper, cayenne, tomatoes and water, stir, cover and cook on High for 3 minutes.

5. Transfer to your blender, leave aside to cool down a bit and pulse until you obtain a paste.

6. Transfer to a bowl and serve for breakfast.

Enjoy!

Nutrition: *calories 100, fat 2, fiber 1, carbs 3, protein 4*

Great Butternut Squash Breakfast

Prep Time	Cook Time	Serving
10 Minutes	8 Minutes	7

Ingredients

6 pounds butternut squash, peeled and cut into chunks
1 cup water
1 cup apple cider
2 cinnamon sticks
1 teaspoon ginger, grated
½ cup honey
A pinch of nutmeg, ground
1 tablespoon apple cider vinegar
A pinch of cloves, ground

Directions

1. Put the water in your instant pot, add the steamer basket and put butternut squash inside.

2. Cover, cook on High for 5 minutes, transfer squash to a bowl and leave aside to cool down.

3. Clean instant pot, add squash, apple cider, cinnamon sticks, ginger, cloves, vinegar, nutmeg and honey, stir, cover and cook on High for 3 minutes more.

4. Discard cinnamon sticks, blend using an immersion blender, transfer to jars and serve cold for breakfast.

Enjoy!

Nutrition:

calories 153, fat 3, fiber 1, carbs 5, protein 7

Special Onion And Bacon Jam

Prep Time	Cook Time	Serving
10 Minutes	25 minutes	6

Ingredients

3 tablespoons bacon fat
2 tablespoons garlic olive oil
4 pounds yellow onions, sliced
½ teaspoon baking soda
½ package bacon, cooked and cut into thin strips
5 garlic cloves, minced
½ cup water
¼ cup balsamic vinegar
1 teaspoon thyme, dried
Black pepper to the taste
1 teaspoon red pepper flakes
2 tablespoons stevia

Directions

1. Put the bacon fat in your instant pot, set on Sauté mode and heat it up.

2. Add onions, stir and sauté for 3 minutes.

3. Add garlic olive oil, baking soda, bacon, garlic, water, vinegar, thyme, black pepper, red pepper flakes and stevia, stir, cover and cook on High for 20 minutes.

4. Uncover the pot, set it on Sauté mode again and cook for 2 minutes more.

5. Stir well, divide into jars and serve for breakfast.

Enjoy!

Nutrition:

calories 254, fat 3, fiber 2, carbs 5, protein 7

Breakfast Apple Spread

Prep Time	Cook Time	Serving
10 Minutes	4 Minutes	10

Ingredients

Juice from 1 lemon

1 teaspoon allspice

1 teaspoon clove, ground

3 pounds apples, peeled, cored and chopped

1 tablespoon cinnamon, ground

1 and ½ cups water

¼ teaspoon nutmeg, ground

1 cup maple syrup

Directions

1. In your slow cooker, mix apples with water, lemon juice, allspice, clove, cinnamon, maple syrup and nutmeg.

2. Stir, cover and cook on High for 4 minutes

3. Blend using an immersion blender, pour into small jars and serve for breakfast!

Enjoy!

Nutrition: *calories 180, fat 3, fiber 1, carbs 4, protein 3*

Simple Breakfast Meatloaf

Prep Time	Cook Time	Serving
10 Minutes	50 Minutes	4

Ingredients

1 onion, chopped
1 and ½ cups water
2 pounds pork, minced
1 teaspoon red pepper flakes
1 teaspoon olive oil
3 garlic cloves, minced
¼ cup almond flour
1 teaspoon oregano, chopped
1 tablespoon sage, minced
A pinch of sea salt and black pepper
1 tablespoon paprika
1 teaspoon marjoram, dried
2 eggs

Directions

1. Set your instant pot on sauté mode, add the oil and heat it up.

2. Add onion and garlic, stir and sauté for 3 minutes.

3. Transfer these to a bowl, leave aside to cool down and mix with the meat.

4. Add a pinch of salt, black pepper, pepper flakes, almond flour, sage, oregano, eggs, paprika and marjoram, stir really well and transfer this to a greased meatloaf pan.

5. Add the water to your instant pot, add the steamer basket, add the meatloaf inside, cover and cook on High for 50 minutes.

6. Leave meatball to cool down, slice, divide among plates and serve for breakfast.

Enjoy!

Nutrition:

calories 210, fat 3, fiber 1, carbs 5, protein 12

Summer Veggie Breakfast

Prep Time	Cook Time	Serving
10 Minutes	10 minutes	4

Ingredients

1 and ½ cups red onion, roughly chopped
1 cup cherry tomatoes, halved
2 cups okra, sliced
1 cup water
1 cup mushrooms, sliced
2 and ½ cups zucchini, roughly chopped
2 cups yellow bell pepper, chopped
Black pepper to the taste
2 tablespoons basil, chopped
1 tablespoon thyme, chopped
½ cup olive oil
½ cup balsamic vinegar

Directions

1. In a large bowl, mix onion with tomatoes, okra, zucchini, bell pepper, mushrooms, basil, thyme, black pepper, oil and vinegar and toss well.

2. Transfer to your instant pot, add 1 cup water, cover and cook on High for 10 minutes.

3. Divide among plates and serve for breakfast.

Enjoy!

Nutrition:

calories 120, fat 2, fiber 2, carbs 3, protein 6

Special Breakfast Butter

Prep Time	Cook Time	Serving
10 Minutes	4 Minutes	10

Ingredients

5 cups blueberries puree
2 teaspoons cinnamon powder
Zest from 1 lemon
1 cup coconut sugar
½ teaspoon nutmeg, ground
¼ teaspoon ginger, ground

Directions

1. Put blueberries puree in your instant pot, cover and cook on High for 3 minutes.

2. Add coconut sugar, ginger, nutmeg and lemon zest, stir, cover and cook on High for 3 minutes more.

3. Stir, transfer to jars, cover and serve for breakfast.

Enjoy!

Nutrition: *calories 123, fat 2, fiber 3, carbs 3, protein 4*

Zucchini And Carrots Delightful Breakfast

Prep Time	Cook Time	Serving
10 Minutes	4 Minutes	4

Ingredients

1 and ½ cups almond milk
A pinch of nutmeg, ground
1 small zucchini, grated
1 carrot, grated
A pinch of cloves, ground
2 tablespoons agave nectar
½ teaspoon cinnamon powder
¼ cup pecans, chopped

Directions

1. Put the milk, zucchini, carrots, nutmeg, cloves, cinnamon and agave nectar in your instant pot, cover and cook on High for 4 minutes.

2. Add pecans, stir gently, divide into bowls and serve for breakfast.

Enjoy!

Nutrition:

calories 100, fat 1, fiber 2, carbs 5, protein 5

Bacon and Sweet Potatoes

Prep Time	Cook Time	Serving
10 Minutes	10 minutes	4

Ingredients

½ cup orange juice
4 bacon slices, cooked and crumbled
4 pounds sweet potatoes, sliced
3 tablespoons agave nectar
½ teaspoon thyme, dried
½ teaspoon sage, crushed
A pinch of sea salt and black pepper
2 tablespoons olive oil

Directions

1. Put sweet potato slices, orange juice, agave nectar, thyme, sage, sea salt, black pepper, olive oil and bacon in your instant pot, cover and cook on High for 10 minutes.

2. Transfer to plates and serve for breakfast.

Enjoy!

Nutrition:

calories 159, fat 4, fiber 4, carbs 5, protein 4

Acorn Squash Breakfast Surprise

Prep Time	Cook Time	Serving
10 Minutes	7 Minutes	4

Ingredients

¼ cup raisins

¼ teaspoon cinnamon powder

14 ounces cranberry sauce, unsweetened

2 acorn squash, peeled and cut into medium chunks

A pinch of sea salt

Black pepper to the taste

Directions

1. In your instant pot, mix squash pieces with sauce, raisins, cinnamon, salt and pepper, stir, cover and cook on High for 7 minutes

2. Divide into medium bowls and serve for breakfast.

Enjoy!

Nutrition: *calories 160, fat 3, fiber 2, carbs 7, protein 5*

Tasty Zucchini And Squash

Prep Time	Cook Time	Serving
10 Minutes	10 Minutes	6

Ingredients

2 cups zucchinis, sliced
2 tablespoons olive oil
1 teaspoon Italian seasoning
Black pepper to the taste
2 cups yellow squash, peeled and cut
into wedges
1 teaspoon garlic powder
A pinch of sea salt

Directions

1. Set your instant pot on sauté mode, add the oil and heat it up.

2. Add squash and zucchinis, stir and sauté for 3 minutes.

3. Add seasoning, garlic powder, salt and black pepper, toss, cover and cook on High for 7 minutes.

4. Divide among plates and serve as a quick breakfast.

Enjoy!

Nutrition:

calories 132, fat 2, fiber 4, carbs 3, protein 4

Breakfast Balls

Prep Time	Cook Time	Serving
10 Minutes	12 minutes	8

Ingredients

2 eggs
1 teaspoon baking soda
1 pound sausage, casings removed
and chopped
¼ cup almond flour
1 cup water
Black pepper to the taste
1 teaspoon smoked paprika

Directions

1. In your food processor, mix sausage with eggs, baking soda, flour, pepper and paprika, pulse well and shape medium balls from this mix.

2. Put the water in your instant pot, add the steamer basket, place meatballs inside, cover and cook on High for 12 minutes.

3. Divide among plates and serve for breakfast.

Enjoy!

Nutrition:

calories 150, fat 3, fiber 3, carbs 6, protein 5

Breakfast Muffins

Prep Time	Cook Time	Serving
10 Minutes	20 Minutes	10

Ingredients

1 cup water

½ teaspoon baking soda

2 and ½ cups almond flour

1 tablespoon vanilla extract

¼ cup coconut oil

¼ cup coconut milk

2 eggs

¼ cup maple syrup

3 tablespoons cinnamon, ground

1 cup blueberries

Directions

1. In a bowl, mix almond flour with baking soda, eggs, oil, coconut milk, cinnamon, maple syrup, vanilla and blueberries, stir everything using your mixer and divide this into silicone muffin cups.

2. Put the water in your instant pot, add the steamer basket, add muffin cups, cover and cook on High for 20 minutes.

3. Divide muffins between plates and serve them for breakfast.

Enjoy!

Nutrition: *calories 170, fat 3, fiber 1, carbs 3, protein 5*

Avocado Muffins

Prep Time	Cook Time	Serving
10 Minutes	30 Minutes	12

Ingredients

1 cup water
6 bacon slices, chopped
A drizzle of olive oil
1 yellow onion, chopped
4 avocados, pitted, peeled and chopped
4 eggs
½ cup almond flour
½ teaspoon baking soda
1 cup almond milk
A pinch of sea salt
Black pepper to the taste

Directions

1. Set your instant pot on Sauté mode, add a drizzle of oil and heat it up.

2. Add onion and bacon, stir, sauté for 3 minutes and transfer to a bowl.

3. Add avocados and mash everything using a fork.

4. Add a pinch of salt, pepper, eggs, baking soda, milk and flour, whisk everything well and divide into silicon muffin tins.

5. Put the water in your instant pot, add the steamer basket, add the muffins inside, cover and cook on High for 25 minutes.

6. Divide among plates and serve for breakfast.

Enjoy!

Nutrition:

calories 180, fat 4, fiber 3, carbs 5, protein 7

Chorizo Breakfast

Prep Time	Cook Time	Serving
10 Minutes	15 minutes	2

Ingredients

1 small avocado, peeled, pitted and chopped
½ cup beef stock
1 pound chorizo, chopped
2 poblano peppers, chopped
1 cup kale, chopped
8 mushrooms, chopped
½ yellow onion, chopped
3 garlic cloves, minced
½ cup cilantro, chopped
4 bacon slices, chopped
4 eggs

Directions

1. Set your instant pot on Brown mode, add bacon and chorizo and cook for a couple of minutes.

2. Add onions, poblano peppers and garlic, stir and sauté for a few more minutes.

3. Add stock, mushrooms and kale and stir.

4. Make holes in this mix, crack an egg in each, cover and cook on High for 3 minutes

5. Divide this mix on plates, sprinkle cilantro and avocado on top and serve for breakfast.

Enjoy!

Nutrition:

calories 170, fat 5, fiber 3, carbs 6, protein 6

Eggs, Ham And Mushroom Mix

Prep Time	Cook Time	Serving
10 Minutes	10 Minutes	1

Ingredients

2 tablespoons ghee

¼ cup coconut milk

3 eggs

3.5 ounces smoked ham, chopped

3 ounces mushrooms, sliced

1 cup arugula, torn

A pinch of black pepper

Directions

1. Set your instant pot on Sauté mode, add the ghee and heat it up.

2. Add mushrooms and ham, stir and cook for 3 minutes.

3. Meanwhile, in a bowl, mix eggs with milk and some black pepper and whisk well.

4. Spread this mix over mushrooms and ham, stir gently, cover and cook on Low for 6 minutes.

5. Divide among plates and serve with arugula on top.

Enjoy!

Nutrition: *calories 156, fat 2, fiber 2, carbs 6, protein 14*

Delicious Nuts And Fruits Breakfast

Prep Time	Cook Time	Serving
10 Minutes	10 Minutes	4

Ingredients

½ cup almonds, soaked for 12 hours and drained
½ cup walnuts, soaked for 12 hours and drained
2 apples, peeled, cored and cubed
1 butternut squash, peeled and cubed
1 teaspoon cinnamon powder
1 tablespoon honey
½ teaspoon nutmeg, ground
1 cup coconut milk

Directions

1. Put almonds and walnuts in your blender, add some of the soaking water, blend well, transfer to your instant pot, add apples, squash, cinnamon, honey, nutmeg and coconut milk, stir, cover and cook on High for 10 minutes

2. Mash everything, divide into bowls and serve for breakfast.

Enjoy!

Nutrition:

calories 140, fat 1, fiber 2, carbs 2, protein 4

Leek and Kale Breakfast

Prep Time	Cook Time	Serving
10 Minutes	10 minutes	4

Ingredients

1 and 1/3 cups leek, chopped
½ cup water
2 tablespoons coconut oil
1 cup kale, chopped
2 teaspoons garlic, minced
8 eggs
2/3 cup sweet potato, grated
1 and ½ cups beef sausage, casings removed and chopped

Directions

1. Put the oil in your instant pot, set on Sauté mode and heat it up.

2. Add leeks, stir and cook for 1 minute.

3. Add garlic, sweet potatoes and kale, stir and sauté for 2 minutes more.

4. Add eggs and sausage meat, stir everything, cover and cook on High for 6 minutes.

5. Divide among plates and serve for breakfast.

Enjoy!

Nutrition:

calories 170, fat 2, fiber 2, carbs 6, protein 6

Snacks

Sweet Potato Fries

Prep Time	Cook Time	Serving
10 Minutes	15 Minutes	2

Ingredients

1lb sweet potato, cut into chips.
2tbsp butter
1tbsp olive oil
1tbsp honey
salt and pepper

Directions

Blanch the potatoes in hot water.

Melt the butter and olive oil in the Instant Pot.

Add the sweet potato and saute until crisp.

Stir in the honey, salt and pepper. Leave to rest.

Nutrition:

Calories: 250 Carbs: 36 Sugar: 17 Fat: 7 Protein: 5

Sugar Oats Cup

Prep Time	Cook Time	Serving
10 Minutes	5 minutes	2

Ingredients

0.5 cup instant oats
2 cups milk
4tbsp brown sugar
1tsp cinnamon

Directions

Pour the milk into your Instant Pot.

Add the oats, sugar, and cinnamon, stir well.

Seal and close the vent.

Choose Manual and set to cook 5 minutes.

Release the pressure naturally.

Nutrition:

Calories: 220 Carbs: 35 Sugar: 11 Fat: 4 Protein: 10

Leek And Potato Soup

Prep Time	Cook Time	Serving
15 Minutes	25 Minutes	2

Ingredients

2 cups chopped white potatoes
2 chopped leeks
1 cups vegetable stock
1 cup black pepper sauce
1 cup chopped cilantro

Directions

Mix all the ingredients in your Instant Pot.

Cook on Stew for 25 minutes.

Depressurize naturally and blend.

Nutrition: *Calories: 220 Carbs: 26 Sugar: 3 Fat: 16 Protein: 5*

Stuffed Apples

Prep Time	Cook Time	Serving
10 Minutes	20 Minutes	2

Ingredients

2 medium cooking apples
2oz blackberries
2tbsp honey
1/2tsp cinnamon

Directions

Core the apples, leaving a little at the base for structure.

Mix the honey, cinnamon, and blackberries, and pack into the apples.

Place the apples in the steamer basket in your Instant Pot.

Pour a cup of water into your Instant Pot.

Seal and cook on Steam 20 minutes.

Depressurize naturally.

Nutrition:

Calories: 129 Carbs: 31 Sugar: 15 Fat: 0 Protein: 1 5

Bread And Butter Pudding

Prep Time	Cook Time	Serving
20 Minutes	20 minutes	2

Ingredients

1 cup single cream
1 large egg
2 slices stale bread
1tbsp brown sugar
1tsp salted butter

Directions

Whisk together the egg, cream, and sugar.

Butter the bread and layer it in a small heat-proof bowl.

Pour the egg mix over the bread. Pour a cup of water into the Instant Pot.

Place the bowl in the steamer basket and the basket in the Instant Pot.

Cook on Steam, low pressure, for 20 minutes.

Depressurize quickly and serve.

Nutrition:

Calories: 560 Carbs: 40 Sugar: 29 Fat: 40 Protein: 9

Honey Oat Boost

Prep Time	Cook Time	Serving
10 Minutes	5 Minutes	2

Ingredients

0.5 cup instant oats
2 cups milk
4tbsp honey
2tbsp very milk chocolate chips

Directions

Pour the milk into your Instant Pot.

Add the oats, chocolate, and 3tbsp honey, stir well.

Seal and close the vent.

Choose Manual and set to cook 5 minutes.

Release the pressure naturally.

Drizzle with more honey.

Nutrition: *Calories: 320 Carbs: 37 Sugar: 16 Fat: 4 Protein: 8*

Eve's Pudding

Prep Time	Cook Time	Serving
30 Minutes	20 Minutes	2

Ingredients

2 large apples, thinly sliced
1 egg
3tbsp plain butter
3tbsp self-raising flour
2tbsp brown sugar

Directions

Grease a heat-proof bowl with a pinch of the butter and layer the apple into it.

Whisk the remaining butter and sugar together until it's blended.

Add in the eggs, then carefully fold in the flour. Spread the batter over the apples.

Pour a cup of water into the Instant Pot.

Place the bowl in the steamer basket and the basket in the Instant Pot.

Cook on Steam, low pressure, for 20 minutes. Depressurize quickly and serve.

Nutrition:

Calories: 600 Carbs: 75 Sugar: 50 Fat: 30 Protein: 9

Juicy Lucy

Prep Time	Cook Time	Serving
20 Minutes	15 minutes	2

Ingredients

2 medium pears, peeled, cored, and quartered
3oz fruits of the forest, fresh or frozen-defrosted
1tbsp blueberry jam
1tbsp cake crumbs
1tbsp brown sugar r

Directions

Mix the fruits with the sugar and jam. Add the pears and mix them.

Put into a heat-proof bowl that fits in your steamer basket in your Instant Pot.

Pour a cup of water into the Instant Pot.

Place the bowl in the steamer basket and the basket in the Instant Pot.

Cook on Steam, low pressure, for 15 minutes. Depressurize quickly.

Mix the crumbs and butter, sprinkle over the pudding and serve.

Nutrition:

Calories: 276 Carbs: 56 Sugar: 16 Fat: 6 Protein: 3

Apple Cake

Prep Time	Cook Time	Serving
20 Minutes	20 Minutes	2

Ingredients

1 large chopped cooking apple
1tbsp flour
1tbsp butter
1 egg
1tsp sugar

Directions

Mix the butter and sugar. Add the egg, then fold in the flour. Fold in the apple.

Lightly grease a heat-proof bowl and pour the batter into the bowl.

Pour a cup of water into the Instant Pot.

Place the bowl in the steamer basket and the basket in the Instant Pot.

Cook on Steam, low pressure, for 20 minutes. Depressurize quickly and serve.

Nutrition: *Calories: 185 Carbs: 22 Sugar: 12 Fat: 8 Protein: 5*

Rice Pudding

Prep Time	Cook Time	Serving
10 Minutes	10 Minutes	2

Ingredients

0.5 cup dry white rice
2 cups milk
4tbsp sugar
1tsp vanilla extract

Directions

Pour the milk into your Instant Pot.

Add the remaining ingredients, stir well.

Seal and close the vent.

Choose Manual and set to cook 10 minutes.

Release the pressure naturally.

Nutrition:

Calories: 320 Carbs: 45 Sugar: 15 Fat: 1 Protein: 2

BBQ Square Ribs

Prep Time	Cook Time	Serving
10 Minutes	20 minutes	3

Ingredients

1 rack pork spare ribs
1 onion, chopped
1 cup apple juice
1 cup bbq sauce
1 teaspoon liquid smoke

Directions

Directions:

In your instant pot, mix spare ribs with onion, apple juice, bbq sauce and liquid smoke, toss, cover and cook on High for 20 minutes.

Arrange ribs on a platter, drizzle bbq sauce all over and serve as an appetizer or snack.

Enjoy!.

Nutrition:

calories 300, fat 8, fiber 5, carbs 12, protein 4

Grated Carrot Appetizer Salad

Prep Time	Cook Time	Serving
10 Minutes	3 Minutes	4

Ingredients

1 pound carrots
1 tablespoon lemon juice
1 teaspoon red pepper flakes
1 tablespoon parsley, chopped
Salt to the taste
For the instant pot
¼ cups water

Directions

In your instant pot, mix carrots with water and salt, cover and cook on High for 3 minutes.

Drain carrots, cool them down, grated and transfer them to a bowl.

Add lemon juice, pepper flakes and parsley, toss, divide into smaller bowls and serve as an appetizer

Enjoy!

Nutrition: *calories 152, fat 3, fiber 3, carbs 4, protein 3*

Green Beans Appetizer Salad

Prep Time	Cook Time	Serving
10 Minutes	2 Minutes	4

Ingredients

pound green beans, trimmed
2 red onions, sliced
1 tablespoon Creole mustard
1 tablespoon red wine vinegar
A drizzle of olive oil
For the instant pot
1 and ½ cups water

Directions

In your instant pot, mix green beans with water, cover and cook on High for 2 minutes.

Drain green beans, transfer to a bowl, add onion slices, mustard, vinegar and oil, toss, divide on appetizer plates and serve as an appetizer.

Enjoy!

Nutrition:

calories 121, fat 4, fiber 4, carbs 6, protein 4

Watercress Appetizer Salad

Prep Time	Cook Time	Serving
10 Minutes	2 minutes	4

Ingredients

1 big bunch watercress, roughly torn
2 peaches, stones removed and cut into medium wedges
1 watermelon, cubed
A drizzle of olive oil
1 tablespoon lemon juice
For the instant pot
½ cups water

Directions

In your instant pot, mix watercress with water, cover and cook on High for 2 minutes.

Drain, transfer to a bowl, add peaches, watermelon, oil and lemon juice, toss, divide on appetizer plates and serve as an appetizer.

Enjoy!

Nutrition:

calories 111, fat 3, fiber 4, carbs 5, protein 3

Ham and Cheese Dip

Prep Time	Cook Time	Serving
10 Minutes	12 Minutes	4

Ingredients

8 ounces cream cheese
1 cup Swiss cheese
1 cup cheddar cheese, grated
2 tablespoons parsley, chopped
8 ham slices, chopped

Directions

Set your instant pot on sauté mode, add ham, stir and brown for 3-4 minutes.

Add Swiss, cheddar and cream cheese, stir, cover and cook on High for 6 minutes.

Add parsley, divide into bowls and serve as an appetizer.

Enjoy!

Nutrition: *calories 243, fat 4, fiber 7, carbs 7, protein 4*

Scallion Spread

Prep Time	Cook Time	Serving
10 Minutes	3 Minutes	6

Ingredients

½ cup scallions, chopped
1 cup sour cream
¼ cup mayonnaise
3 tablespoons dill, chopped
1 tablespoon lemon zest, grated

Directions

Set your instant pot on sauté mode, add scallions, stir and brown for 1 minute.

Add sour cream, stir, cover and cook on High for 2 minutes.

Leave this mix to cool down, add mayo, dill and lemon zest, stir well, divide into bowls and serve with tortilla chips on the side.

Enjoy!

Nutrition:

calories 222, fat 4, fiber 5, carbs 8, protein 4

Crab Spread

Prep Time	Cook Time	Serving
10 Minutes	15 minutes	4

Ingredients

8 ounces crab meat
½ cup sour cream
¼ cup half and half
½ bunch scallions, chopped
1 teaspoon Worcestershire sauce

Directions

In your instant pot, mix crab meat with sour cream, half-and-half, scallions and Worcestershire sauce, stir, cover and cook on High for 15 minutes.

Leave spread to cool down, divide into bowls and serve as an appetizer.

Enjoy!

Nutrition:

calories 241, fat 4, fiber 6, carbs 8, protein 3

Shrimp and Tomatoes Appetizer Mix

Prep Time	Cook Time	Serving
10 Minutes	4 Minutes	6

Ingredients

1 and ½ cups onion, chopped

2 tablespoons butter

15 ounces canned tomatoes, chopped

1 pound shrimp, shelled

1 cup feta cheese, crumbled

Directions

Set your instant pot on sauté mode, add butter, melt it, add onion, stir and cook for 2 minutes.

Add shrimp and tomatoes, toss a bit, cover and cook on Low for 2 minutes.

Divide shrimp and tomatoes mix into small bowls and serve as an appetizer with feta cheese on top.

Enjoy!

Nutrition: *calories 201, fat 3, fiber 4, carbs 7, protein 4*

Tomatoes Appetizer Salad

Prep Time	Cook Time	Serving
10 Minutes	30 Minutes	6

Ingredients

8 beets, trimmed
1 pint mixed cherry tomatoes, halved
1 cup apple cider vinegar
1 red onion, chopped
2 teaspoons sugar
For the instant pot
1 and ½ cups water

Directions

Put the water in your instant pot, add steamer basket, add beets inside, cover and cook on High for 20 minutes.

Drain beets, cool them down, peel, grate them and transfer to a bowl.

Clean the pot, set on sauté mode, add mixed cherries and sugar, toss them and cook for a couple of minutes.

Add onion and vinegar, stir and cook for 2 minutes more.

Add beets, stir, sauté everything for another 2 minutes, divide everything on appetizer plates and serve.

Enjoy!

Nutrition:

calories 118, fat 3, fiber 2, carbs 5, protein 3

Kale and Carrots Salad

Prep Time	Cook Time	Serving
10 Minutes	7 minutes	4

Ingredients

10 ounces kale, roughly chopped
3 carrots, sliced
½ cup chicken stock
1 tablespoon olive oil
1 red onion, chopped

Directions

Set your instant pot on sauté mode, add oil, heat it up, add onion and carrots, stir and cook for 1-2 minutes.

Add kale and stock, stir a bit, cover and cook on High for 5 minutes.

Divide into small bowls and serve as an appetizer.

Enjoy!

Nutrition:

calories 128, fat 2, fiber 4, carbs 8, protein 4

Kale and Wild Rice Appetizer Salad

Prep Time	Cook Time	Serving
10 Minutes	4 Minutes	4

Ingredients

1 cup wild rice, already cooked

1 avocado, peeled, pitted and chopped

1 kale bunch, roughly chopped

1 teaspoon olive oil

3 ounces goat cheese, crumbled

Directions

Set your instant pot on sauté mode, add oil, heat it up, add rice and toast it for 2-3 minutes stirring often.

Add kale, stir, cover and cook on Manual for 2 minutes.

Add avocado, toss, divide on appetizer plates, sprinkle cheese on top and serve.

Enjoy!

Nutrition: *calories 182, fat 3, fiber 2, carbs 4, protein 3*

Minty Kale Salad

Prep Time	Cook Time	Serving
10 Minutes	3 Minutes	4

Ingredients

1 bunch kale, roughly chopped
1 teaspoon sesame oil
2 tablespoons lemon juice
1 cup pineapple, chopped
2 tablespoons mint, chopped

Directions

Set your instant pot on sauté mode, add oil, heat it up, add kale, stir and cook for 1 minute.

Add pineapple, lemon juice and mint, toss, divide on appetizer plates and serve.

Enjoy!

Nutrition:

calories 121, fat 1, fiber 2, carbs 4, protein 2

Broccoli Appetizer Salad

Prep Time	Cook Time	Serving
10 Minutes	10 minutes	4

Ingredients

1 broccoli head, florets separated
½ cup almonds, chopped
2 tablespoons olive oil
¼ cup apple juice
2 tablespoons tamari sauce
For the instant pot
1 and ½ cups water

Directions

Put the water in your instant pot, add steamer basket, add broccoli florets, cover, cook on High for 4 minutes, drain and transfer to a bowl.

Clean the pot, set it on sauté mode, add oil, heat it up, add kale, stir and cook for 2 minutes.

Return broccoli, also add, apple juice and tamari, stir, cover and cook on High for 2 minutes more.

Add almonds, toss, divide into bowls and serve as an appetizer.

Enjoy!

Nutrition:

calories 192, fat 2, fiber 4, carbs 7, protein 4

Little Smokies

Prep Time	Cook Time	Serving
10 Minutes	4 Minutes	4

Ingredients

12 ounces Packages Cocktail Sausages
4 ounces Barbecue Sauce
2 tablespoons of Brown Sugar
½ tablespoon of White Vinegar
2 ounces Beer

Directions

Open the instant pot and add sausage to it.

Then add BBQ sauce, sugar, white vinegar, and beer.

Set the pot setting low and pressure cook for 1 minute.

Once the timer beeps, natural release the steam for 5 minutes.

Then quickly release the steam.

Now if the sauce is not thickened enough turn on the sauté mode and re-cook for 4 minutes.

Once done serve and enjoy.

Nutrition: *Calories1332 Total Fat 102.2g1 Total Carbohydrate 42.4g Protein 60.1g*

Instant Pot Five Ingredients Salsa

Prep Time	Cook Time	Serving
15 Minutes	25 Minutes	2

Ingredients

2 cups fresh tomatoes
4 large yellow onions, chopped & diced
1 cup seeded & chopped jalapeno peppers roasted
1/4 cup vinegar
Salt and black pepper, to taste

Directions

Combine all ingredients in the Instant Pot.

Cook it on high pressure for 25 minutes.

Then use a quick release Directions.

Once done, refrigerate to let it get cold.

Then serve.

Nutrition:

Calories206 Total Fat 1.7g Total Carbohydrate 44.9g Protein 6.7g

Bacon Cheeseburger Dip

Prep Time	Cook Time	Serving
15 Minutes	15 minutes	1

Ingredients

½ pound lean ground beef
4 slices of bacon cut into pieces
5 ounces diced tomatoes
4 ounces cream cheese, cut into cubes
1 cup of tortilla chips
For instant pot:
2 tablespoons water

Directions

Turn on the sauté mode of instant pot and when it reads hot, add bacon and cook for 2 minutes.

Then add the beef by taking out the bacon from the pot.

Cook beef for 7 minutes until brown.

Now add bacon, water, and cream cheese to the pot.

Place lid on top and then turn into sealing.

Cook on high pressure for 5 minutes.

Release the steam quickly.

Stir and then serve with tortilla chips.

Enjoy.

Nutrition:

Calories1775 Total Fat 110.6g1 Total Carbohydrate 79.4g Protein 115.1g

Jalapeno Hot Popper & Chicken Instant Pot Dip

Prep Time	Cook Time	Serving
15 Minutes	15 Minutes	1

Ingredients

½ pound boneless chicken breast
3 ounces cheddar cheese
3/4 cup sour cream
1/4 cup Panko bread crumbs
Salt and black pepper, to taste
For instant pot:
1/4 cup of water

Directions

Open the pot and add chicken breast, salt, pepper and water in it.

Cook for 10 minutes at high pressure.

Then release the steam naturally and open the pot.

Shred the chicken and then stir in cheddar cheese and sour cream.

Now place the mixture into the baking dish and then add Panko bread crumbs on top.

Broil for 4 minters in the oven.

Then serve and enjoy.

Nutrition: *Calories1646 Total Fat 122.1g1 Total Carbohydrate 31g Protein 104.4g*

Instant Pot Cocktail Weiner

Prep Time	Cook Time	Serving
15 Minutes	2Minutes	1

Ingredients

4 ounces of cocktail wieners
6 ounces of BBQ sauce
1/3 Cup water
1 tablespoon of Sriracha

Directions

Pour the BBQ sauce on the bottom of the pot.

Now pour water and then add cocktail wieners and Sriracha sauce.

Close the lid.

Cook on high pressure for 2 minutes.

Now open the pot by releasing the steam by a quick release Directions.

Serve.

Nutrition:

Calories746 Total Fat 36.5g Total Carbohydrate 88.7g Protein 12g

Instant Pot Popcorn

Prep Time	Cook Time	Serving
15 Minutes	4 minutes	1

Ingredients

1 tablespoon of butter
1-1/2 tablespoon of coconut oil
½ cup of popcorn kernels

Directions

Turn on the sauté mode of the instant pot.

Add oil and butter, and allow it to melt.

Once it starts to sizzle, add popcorn and stir to coat well.

Place the lid of the instant pot on top, so it holds the popcorn instead while popping.

Do not lock the lid.

When all the popcorn popped.

Transfer to serving bowl.

Repeat for the next batch.

Once all the popcorns are popped, serve.

Nutrition:

Calories284 Total Fat 27.6g Total Carbohydrate 9g Protein 1.1g

Easy Bacon Hot Dog Bites

Prep Time	Cook Time	Serving
15 Minutes	8 Minutes	1

Ingredients

200 grams of Hot Dogs
¼ jar of grape jelly
4 tablespoons of cocktail sauce
2 slices of Smoked Bacon

Directions

Cut the bacon and hot dogs.

Set the hot dogs aside and then turn on the sauté mode.

Cook bacon for 3 minutes in the instant pot, and then separates the grease from the pot.

Now add hot dog in the pot.

Now add jelly and cocktail sauce.

Turn off the sauté mode.

Now cook it on high pressure for 4 minutes.

Then quick release steam.

Turn off the pot and transfer it to the serving dish.

Enjoy.

Nutrition: *Calories935 Total Fat 75.5g Total Carbohydrate 22.1g Protein 37.6g*

Nuts in Instant Pot

Prep Time	Cook Time	Serving
15 Minutes	20 Minutes	2

Ingredients

1 cup pecan halves
4 tablespoons of maple syrup
1/4 tablespoon vanilla extract
1/2 teaspoon nutmeg
1/2 teaspoon salt
For instant pot:
1/4 cup of water

Directions

Turn on the sauté mode of the instant pot and add pecans, maple syrup, water, vanilla, nutmeg, and salt to it.

Sauté the ingredients for a few minutes, once the pecans get tender turn off the sauté mode.

Now add water to the pot and select the cooking time to 10 minutes at high pressure

Meanwhile, preheat the oven to 350 degrees F.

Once the timer beeps, transfer the pecan to the baking sheet.

Bake in preheated oven for 3 minutes, then take out and flip to cook from the other side.

Now again place it in the oven and cook for the additional 3 minutes.

Once done, let it get cool, then serve.

Nutrition:

Calories1089 Total Fat 100.3g1 Total Carbohydrate 48g Protein 15.1g

---

Classic Wings

Prep Time	Cook Time	Serving
15 Minutes	20 minutes	1

Ingredients

1 pound chicken wings cleaned and halved
¼ cup honey
¼ cup low sodium soy sauce
½ tablespoon vegetable oil
1 clove of garlic, minced

Directions

Take a medium bowl, and mix the honey, soy sauce, garlic, and the oil in it.

Marinate the chicken in it, for few hours.

Now, pour the prepared sauce along with the chicken in the instant pot

Cook on high for 20 minutes.

Once done, release the steam naturally.

Open and serve the chicken.

Nutrition:

Calories1671 Total Fat 95.1g1 Saturated Fat 26.1g1 Cholesterol 381mg1 Sodium 2501mg1 Total Carbohydrate 76.3g Dietary Fiber 0.7g Total Sugars 70.7g Protein 125.6g Vitamin D 0mcg Calcium 89mg Iron 7mg Potassium 1005mg

Simple Wings

Prep Time	Cook Time	Serving
15 Minutes	25 Minutes	1

Ingredients

1 pound chicken wings
2 tablespoons of honey
¼ teaspoon ground ginger
¼ teaspoon garlic powder
Salt to taste

Directions

Combine all the ingredients in an instant pot, and close the lid.

Now, set the timer to 15 minutes.

Once the timer beeps, quick release steam.

Now layer the chicken onto the baking sheet, and bake in oven at 350 degrees F, for 10 minutes.

Once the top is browned, serve and enjoy.

Nutrition: *Calories1038 Total Fat 33.7g Saturated Fat 9.3g Cholesterol 404mg1 Sodium 5339mg2 Total Carbohydrate 41.9g Dietary Fiber 0.9g Total Sugars 36.1g Protein 136.9g Vitamin D 0mcg Calcium 88mg Iron 7mg Potassium 1322mg*

Tasty Black Bean Salsa

Prep Time	Cook Time	Serving
10 Minutes	8 Minutes	4

Ingredients

1 small white onion, chopped
8 ounces canned black beans, drained
2 tablespoons lime juice
1 tablespoon olive oil
2 red jalapenos, chopped

Directions

Set your instant pot on sauté mode, add oil, heat it up, add onion, stir and cook for 2-3 minutes.

Add black beans, lime juice and jalapenos, stir, cover and cook on High for 3 minutes.

Divide into bowls and serve warm.

Enjoy!

Nutrition:

calories 172, fat 3, fiber 4, carbs 6, protein 3

Special Ranch Spread

Prep Time	Cook Time	Serving
10 Minutes	10 minutes	12

Ingredients

1 cup sour cream
1 pound bacon, chopped
1 cup mayonnaise
1 cup Monterey jack cheese, shredded
4 green onions, chopped

Directions

Set your instant pot on sauté mode, add bacon, stir and cook until it is crispy.

Add sour cream and green onions, stir, cover and cook on High for 6 minutes.

Add cheese and mayo, stir well, leave aside for a few minutes, divide into bowls and serve as an appetizer.

Enjoy!

Nutrition:

calories 261, fat 4, fiber 6, carbs 7, protein 4

Chicken Dip

Prep Time	Cook Time	Serving
10 Minutes	15 Minutes	6

Ingredients

3 cups chicken, cooked and shredded

4 ounces cream cheese

1 cup mozzarella cheese, shredded

½ cup hot sauce

1 cup Greek yogurt

Directions

In your instant pot, mix chicken with cream cheese and hot sauce, stir, cover and cook on High for 15 minutes.

Add yogurt and mozzarella, stir, leave aside for a few minutes, divide into bowls and serve as an appetizer.

Enjoy!

Nutrition: *calories 188, fat 4, fiber 7, carbs 8, protein 4*

Blue Cheese Dip

Prep Time	Cook Time	Serving
10 Minutes	4 Minutes	6

Ingredients

4 tablespoons blue cheese, crumbled
1 cup sour cream
2 tablespoons chives, chopped
1 and ½ teaspoons rosemary, chopped
Black pepper to the taste

Directions

In your instant pot, mix blue cheese with sour cream, rosemary and black pepper, stir, cover and cook on Manual for 4 minutes.

Add chives, whisk dip, divide into bowls and serve as an appetizer.

Enjoy!

Nutrition:

calories 200, fat 7, fiber 5, carbs 7, protein 4

Chunky Warm Salsa

Prep Time	Cook Time	Serving
10 Minutes	4 minutes	5

Ingredients

1 red bell pepper, cut into medium pieces
2 peaches, roughly chopped
1 red onion, roughly chopped
A drizzle of olive oil
2 tablespoons lime juice

Directions

Set your instant pot on sauté mode, add oil, heat it up, add onion, stir and cook for 1 minute.

Add red pepper, peaches and lime juice, toss, cover and cook on High for 3 minutes.

Leave this appetizer to cool down, divide into small bowls and serve.

Enjoy!

Nutrition:

calories 152, fat 2, fiber 3, carbs 4, protein 4

Cumin Dip

Prep Time	Cook Time	Serving
10 Minutes	2 Minutes	4

Ingredients

1 cup sour cream

1/3 cup mayonnaise

1 and ¼ teaspoon cumin, ground

1 tablespoon hot sauce

1 tablespoon lime juice

Directions

In your instant pot, mix sour cream with cumin and hot sauce, stir, cover and cook on High for 2 minutes.

Leave dip to cool down, add mayo and lime juice, stir, divide into bowls and serve.

Enjoy!

Nutrition: *calories 209, fat 6, fiber 3, carbs 7, protein 7*

Pinto Bean Dip

Prep Time	Cook Time	Serving
10 Minutes	8 Minutes	4

Ingredients

8 ounces canned pinto beans, drained
4 rosemary sprigs, chopped
1 and ¼ cup parsley, chopped
3 tablespoons lemon juice
2 tablespoons tomatoes, chopped

Directions

In your instant pot, mix pinto beans with rosemary and tomatoes, stir, cover and cook on High for 8 minutes.

Blend using an immersion blender, add parsley and lemon juice, stir again, divide into bowls and serve as an appetizer.

Enjoy!

Nutrition:

calories 272, fat 3, fiber 8, carbs 9, protein 8

Light Lemon Dip

Prep Time	Cook Time	Serving
10 Minutes	10 minutes	6

Ingredients

2 lemons, roasted in the oven and pulp separated
1 tablespoon olive oil
1 cup sour cream
½ cup chives, chopped
1 cup mayonnaise

Directions

In your instant pot, mix lemon pulp with sour cream and oil, whisk well, cover and cook on High for 5 minutes.

Leave aside dip to cool down, add chives and mayo, whisk well, divide into bowls and serve as an appetizer.

Enjoy!

Nutrition:

calories 200, fat 3, fiber 4, carbs 6, protein 8

Green Olive Pate

Prep Time	Cook Time	Serving
10 Minutes	2 Minutes	4

Ingredients

2 cups green olives, pitted
2 anchovy fillets
2 garlic cloves, minced
1 tablespoon capers, chopped
½ cup olive oil

Directions

In a food processor, mix olives with anchovy fillets, garlic, capers and olive oil, pulse well, transfer to your instant pot, cover and cook on High for 2 minutes.

Divide into bowls and serve cold as an appetizer.

Enjoy!

Nutrition: *calories 118, fat 2, fiber 2, carbs 5, protein 4*

Desserts And
Beverages

Pear and Cranberry Cake

Prep Time	Cook Time	Serving
10 Minutes	35 Minutes	6

Ingredients

1 cup chopped pear

1/2 cup chopped cranberries, fresh

1 1/4 cup pastry flour, whole-wheat

2 tablespoons ground flax seeds

1/4 cup agave syrup

Directions

Place flour in a bowl, add 1/8 teaspoon salt, 1/2 teaspoon baking powder, 1/2 teaspoon soda, and 1/2 teaspoon cardamom and stir until mixed.

Pour 1/2 cup almond milk in another bowl, add agave syrup, flax seeds and 2 tablespoons oil and whisk until combined.

Gradually whisk in flour mixture until smooth and incorporated and then fold in pear and cranberries until mixed.

Take a Bundt pan, about 7-inch, grease with oil, then spoon in the prepared batter and cover the pan with a foil.

Switch on the instant pot, pour in 1 1/2 cups water in the inner pot, insert steamer rack and place Bundt pan on it.

Secure instant pot with its lid in the sealed position, then press the manual button, adjust cooking time to 35 minutes, select high-pressure cooking and let cook until instant pot buzz.

Instant pot will take 10 minutes or more to build pressure, and when it buzzes, press the cancel button and do natural pressure release for 10 minutes or more until pressure knob drops down.

Then carefully open the instant pot, take out the pan, uncover it, and slice to serve.

Nutrition: *Calories: 259 Cal Carbs: 48 g Fat: 6 g Protein: 4 g Fiber: 6 g*

Peach Dump Cake

Prep Time	Cook Time	Serving
10 Minutes	15 Minutes	8

Ingredients

1 cup sliced peaches, deseeded and skin on

21-ounce peach pie filling

15-ounce yellow cake mix

½ cup vegan butter, sliced

Directions

Switch on the instant pot, pour 1 cup water in the inner pot and insert trivet stand.

Place peach slices in a heatproof bowl that fits in the instant pot, add peach pie filling along with peaches, sprinkle with 1 tablespoon brown sugar and ½ teaspoon cinnamon and toss until well coated.

Top peach filling with cake mix, scatter with sliced butter, cover the bowl with aluminum foil and place on the trivet stand.

Secure instant pot with its lid in the sealed position, then press the manual button, adjust cooking time to 10 minutes, select high-pressure cooking and let cook until instant pot buzz.

Instant pot will take 10 minutes or more to build pressure, and when it buzzes, press the cancel button and do natural pressure release for 10 minutes or more until pressure knob drops down.

When the cake is done, carefully open the instant pot and take out the cake bowl.

Place the bowl under the broiler and cook for 3 to 5 minutes or until the top is nicely golden brown.

Serve cake with vegan ice cream.

Nutrition:

Calories: 245 Cal Carbs: 43 g Fat: 7.3 g Protein: 2.3 g Fiber: 1.2 g

---

Apple Crisp

Prep Time	Cook Time	Serving
10 Minutes	12 minutes	4

Ingredients

5 cups sliced apples

1 1/2 cups Sprouted Oat and Vanilla Chia Granola

2 tablespoons maple syrup

1/2 lemon, zested

1 teaspoon vanilla extract

Directions

Place granola in a heatproof bowl that fits into the instant pot, then add 1/4 cup coconut oil, 2 tablespoons coconut sugar, ½ teaspoon ginger, and granola mixture and stir until well combined.

Place apples in another bowl, add 2 tablespoons coconut sugar along with remaining ingredients, then stir until mixed and layer apples on top of granola mixture.

Switch on the instant pot, pour 2/3 cup water in the inner pot, insert the trivet stand and place bowl on it.

Secure instant pot with its lid in the sealed position, then press the manual button, adjust cooking time to 2 minutes, select high-pressure cooking and let cook until instant pot buzz.

Instant pot will take 10 minutes or more to build pressure, and when it buzzes, press the cancel button and do quick pressure release until pressure knob drops down.

Meanwhile, stir together ¾ teaspoon cinnamon and lemon zest until well mixed.

Then carefully open the instant pot, take out the bowl, let it sit for 5 minutes and then garnish with lemon zest-cinnamon mixture.

Serve immediately with coconut whipped cream.

Nutrition:

Calories: 293 Cal Carbs: 43.1 g Fat: 13.3 g Protein: 2 g Fiber: 4.5 g

Carrot Cake

Prep Time	Cook Time	Serving
10 Minutes	50 Minutes	4

Ingredients

1 cup shredded carrot

1 cup chopped dates

1 1/2 cups pastry flour, whole-wheat

2 tablespoons ground flax seed, mixed with 1/4 cup warm water

1/2 teaspoon vanilla extract

Directions

Place flour in a bowl, add 1/4 teaspoon salt, 1/4 teaspoon ground ginger, 3/4 teaspoon baking powder, 3/4 teaspoon baking soda, 1/4 teaspoon ground allspice, 1/2 teaspoon ground cinnamon, and 1/4 teaspoon ground cardamom and stir well until mixed.

Pour 1/2 cup almond milk in another bowl, add flaxseed mixture along with 1/4 cup avocado and vanilla and stir well until smooth.

Then gradually whisk in flour mixture until smooth and incorporated batter comes together, fold in dates and carrots until mixed, then spoon the batter into a cake pan that fits into the instant pot and cover the pan with aluminum foil.

Switch on the instant pot, pour 1 1/2 cups water in the inner pot, insert the trivet stand and place the covered cake pan on it.

Secure instant pot with its lid in the sealed position, then press the manual button, adjust cooking time to 50 minutes, select high-pressure cooking and let cook until instant pot buzz.

Instant pot will take 10 minutes or more to build pressure, and when it buzzes, press the cancel button and do natural pressure release for 10 minutes or more until pressure knob drops down.

When the cake is done, carefully open the instant pot, take out the cake pan, let the cake cool for 10 minutes in the cake pan and then take it out.

Slice and serve.

Nutrition: *Calories: 374 Cal Carbs: 68 g Fat: 9 g Protein: 11 g Fiber: 9 g*

Double Chocolate Cake

Prep Time	Cook Time	Serving
10 Minutes	30 Minutes	6

Ingredients

1½ teaspoons ground flaxseeds, mixed with 2 teaspoons warm water
1 cup all-purpose flour
⅔ cup cocoa powder
½ teaspoon vanilla extract
1 cup almond milk, unsweetened

Directions

Place flour in another bowl, add cocoa powder, ½ teaspoon baking powder, ⅛ teaspoon sea salt, ¼ teaspoon baking soda, ⅔ cup coconut sugar and stir until combined.

Then gradually whisk this mixture into the milk and vanilla until smooth and incorporated.

Spoon the batter into a 6 by 3-inch springform pan and smooth the top with a spatula.

Switch on the instant pot, pour 1 ½ cup water in the inner pot, insert a trivet stand and place cake pan on it.

Secure instant pot with its lid in the sealed position, then press the manual button, adjust cooking time to 90 minutes, select high-pressure cooking and let cook until instant pot buzz.

Instant pot will take 10 minutes or more to build pressure, and when it buzzes, press the cancel button and do natural pressure release for 10 minutes or more until pressure knob drops down.

When the cake is done, carefully open the instant pot, take out the pan, and let the cake cool for 10 minutes and then chill cake in the refrigerator for 20 minutes.

Slice and serve.

Nutrition:

Calories: 217.8Cal
Carbs: 27.3 g Fat: 10.5 g Protein: 3.7 g Fiber: 2.4 g

Pumpkin Spice Cake

Prep Time	Cook Time	Serving
10 Minutes	15 minutes	6

Ingredients

3/4 cup buckwheat flour
¼ teaspoon pumpkin pie spice
1 teaspoon apple cider vinegar
¼ cup pumpkin puree
1/3 cup almond milk, unsweetened

Directions

Place flour in a large bowl, add 1 teaspoon baking powder, 2 tablespoons coconut oil, ½ teaspoon vanilla extract, 1/3 cup maple syrup along with remaining ingredients and whisk until incorporated and smooth batter comes together.

Spoon the batter into a cake pan that fits into the instant pot and smooth the top.

Switch on the instant pot, pour 2 cups water in the inner pot, insert a trivet stand and place cake pan on it.

Secure instant pot with its lid in the sealed position, then press the manual button, adjust cooking time to 15 minutes, select high-pressure cooking and let cook until instant pot buzz.

Instant pot will take 10 minutes or more to build pressure, and when it buzzes, press the cancel button and do natural pressure release for 10 minutes or more until pressure knob drops down.

Then carefully open the instant pot, take out the pan, and let cool.

Slice to serve.

Nutrition:

Calories: 195 Cal Carbs: 28.9 g Fat: 7.5 g Protein: 4.3 g Fiber: 5.3 g

Brown Rice Pudding

Prep Time	Cook Time	Serving
10 Minutes	22 Minutes	6

Ingredients

1 cup brown rice, rinsed

2 tablespoons raisins

¼ cup maple syrup

½ teaspoon vanilla extract

2 cups coconut milk, unsweetened

Directions

Switch on the instant pot, place rice in the inner pot, season with 1/8 teaspoon sea salt and ¼ teaspoon ground cinnamon, then add remaining ingredients, and stir well.

Secure instant pot with its lid in the sealed position, then press the manual button, adjust cooking time to 22 minutes, select high-pressure cooking and let cook until instant pot buzz.

Instant pot will take 10 minutes or more to build pressure, and when it buzzes, press the cancel button and do natural pressure release for 10 minutes or more until pressure knob drops down.

Then carefully open the instant pot, stir the pudding, and serve.

Nutrition: *Calories: 170 Cal Carbs: 35.6 g Fat: 1.9 g Protein: 2.9 g Fiber: 1.3 g*

Baked Apples

Prep Time	Cook Time	Serving
10 Minutes	8 Minutes	2

Ingredients

2 large red apples
2 teaspoons raisins
4 teaspoons coconut sugar
1 cup water

Directions

Wash and pat dry apples and core them with a spoon

Switch on the instant pot, pour water in the inner pot, insert a trivet stand, then place apples on it, sprinkle with sugar and top with raisins.

Secure instant pot with its lid in the sealed position, then press the manual button, adjust cooking time to 8 minutes, select high-pressure cooking and let cook until instant pot buzz.

Instant pot will take 10 minutes or more to build pressure, and when it buzzes, press the cancel button, do natural pressure release for 10 minutes and do quick pressure release until pressure knob drops down.

Then carefully open the instant pot, take out the apples, and serve.

Nutrition:

Calories: 99 Cal Carbs: 24.3 g Fat: 0.2 g Protein: 0.4 g Fiber: 2.6 g

---

Pumpkin Oatmeal

Prep Time	Cook Time	Serving
10 Minutes	5 minutes	2

Ingredients

3/4 cup buckwheat flour
¼ teaspoon pumpkin pie spice
1 teaspoon apple cider vinegar
¼ cup pumpkin puree
1/3 cup almond milk, unsweetened

Directions

Pour the milk into your Instant Pot.

Add the remaining ingredients, stir well. Seal and close the vent.

Choose Manual and set to cook 5 minutes. Release the pressure naturally.

Nutrition:

Calories: 320 Carbs: 14 Sugar: 2 Fat: 2 Protein: 3

White Chocolate

Prep Time	Cook Time	Serving
2 Minutes	2 Minutes	2

Ingredients

4tbsp double cream

6tsp powdered sweetener

3tsp sugar-free white chocolate mix

hot water or fat-free milk

Directions

Mix all the ingredients in your Instant Pot.

Seal and cook on Stew for 2 minutes.

Depressurize naturally. Stir well and serve.

Nutrition: *Calories: 105 Carbs: 3 Sugar: 1 Fat: 12 Protein: 4*

Baked Apples

Prep Time	Cook Time	Serving
10 Minutes	8 Minutes	2

Ingredients

2 large red apples
2 teaspoons raisins
4 teaspoons coconut sugar
1 cup water

Directions

Wash and pat dry apples and core them with a spoon

Switch on the instant pot, pour water in the inner pot, insert a trivet stand, then place apples on it, sprinkle with sugar and top with raisins.

Secure instant pot with its lid in the sealed position, then press the manual button, adjust cooking time to 8 minutes, select high-pressure cooking and let cook until instant pot buzz.

Instant pot will take 10 minutes or more to build pressure, and when it buzzes, press the cancel button, do natural pressure release for 10 minutes and do quick pressure release until pressure knob drops down.

Then carefully open the instant pot, take out the apples, and serve.

Nutrition:

Calories: 99 Cal Carbs: 24.3 g Fat: 0.2 g Protein: 0.4 g Fiber: 2.6 g

Pumpkin Oatmeal

Prep Time	Cook Time	Serving
10 Minutes	5 minutes	2

Ingredients

3/4 cup buckwheat flour
¼ teaspoon pumpkin pie spice
1 teaspoon apple cider vinegar
¼ cup pumpkin puree
1/3 cup almond milk, unsweetened

Directions

Pour the milk into your Instant Pot.

Add the remaining ingredients, stir well. Seal and close the vent.

Choose Manual and set to cook 5 minutes. Release the pressure naturally.

Nutrition:

Calories: 320 Carbs: 14 Sugar: 2 Fat: 2 Protein: 3

Hot Chocolate

Prep Time	Cook Time	Serving
2 Minutes	2 Minutes	2

Ingredients

4tbsp double cream
6tsp powdered sweetener
3tsp sugar-free cocoa
1/4tsp vanilla extract
hot water or fat-free milk

Directions

Mix all the ingredients in your Instant Pot.

Seal and cook on Stew for 2 minutes.

Depressurize naturally.

Stir well and serve.

Nutrition: *Calories: 100 Carbs: 3 Sugar: 1 Fat: 11 Protein: 4*

Rich Wild Rice Pudding

Prep Time	Cook Time	Serving
10 Minutes	10 Minutes	2

Ingredients

1/4 cup dry wild rice
1 cup milk
6 squares 90% dark chocolate
4tbsp sweetener
1tsp mixed spice

Directions

Pour the milk into your Instant Pot.

Add the remaining ingredients, stir well.

Seal and close the vent.

Choose Manual and set to cook 10 minutes.

Release the pressure naturally.

Nutrition:

Calories: 320 Carbs: 14 Sugar: 2 Fat: 2 Protein: 3

Peanut Butter Cookies

Prep Time	Cook Time	Serving
10 Minutes	5 minutes	2

Ingredients

1/3 cup peanut butter
1/3 cup dark chocolate chips
2tbsp powdered sweetener
1tbsp applesauce
pinch of baking soda

Directions

Mix the sweetener, applesauce, and baking soda together.

Add in the peanut butter.

Fold in the chocolate chips.

Make cookies and lay them out on a heat-proof tray that fits into your Instant Pot steamer tray.

Pour a cup of water into the Instant Pot.

Place the tray in the steamer basket and the basket in the Instant Pot.

Cook on Steam, low pressure, for 20 minutes.

Depressurize quickly and serve.

Nutrition:

Calories: 390 Carbs: 20 Sugar: 9 Fat: 26 Protein: 10

Chia Pudding With Mango

Prep Time	Cook Time	Serving
10 Minutes	10 Minutes	2

Ingredients

1/4 cup chia seeds
1 cup orange juice
1 cup chopped mango
4tbsp sweetener

Directions

Pour the milk into your Instant Pot.

Add the remaining ingredients, stir well.

Seal and close the vent.

Choose Manual and set to cook 10 minutes.

Release the pressure naturally.

Nutrition: *Calories: 320 Carbs: 12 Sugar: 5 Fat: 6 Protein: 8*

Low Carb Custard

Prep Time	Cook Time	Serving
5 Minutes	20 Minutes	2

Ingredients

2 eggs
2oz cream cheese
1.5tbsp powdered sweetener
1.5tsp caramel sauce
1 cup water

Directions

Blend the ingredients together.

Pour into a heat-proof bowl that fits into your Instant Pot.

Pour a cup of water into the Instant Pot.

Place the bowl in the steamer basket and the basket in the Instant Pot.

Cook on Steam, low pressure, for 20 minutes.

Depressurize quickly and serve.

Nutrition:

Calories: 273 Carbs: 1.5 Sugar: 0 Fat: 27 Protein: 9

Chia Vanilla Pudding

Prep Time	Cook Time	Serving
10 Minutes	10 minutes	2

Ingredients

1/4 cup chia seeds
2 cups milk
4tbsp sweetener
1tsp vanilla extract

Directions

Pour the milk into your Instant Pot.

Add the remaining ingredients, stir well.

Seal and close the vent.

Choose Manual and set to cook 10 minutes.

Release the pressure naturally.

Nutrition:

Calories: 320 Carbs: 11 Sugar: 6 Fat: 6 Protein: 8

Chili Chocolate

Prep Time	Cook Time	Serving
2 Minutes	2 Minutes	2

Ingredients

4tbsp double cream
3tsp powdered sweetener
3tsp sugar-free pure cocoa
1/8tsp chili powder
hot water or fat-free milk

Directions

Mix all the ingredients in your Instant Pot.

Seal and cook on Stew for 2 minutes.

Depressurize naturally.

Stir well and serve.

Nutrition: *Calories: 100 Carbs: 3 Sugar: 1 Fat: 11 Protein: 4*

Bran Porridge

Prep Time	Cook Time	Serving
10 Minutes	10 Minutes	2

Ingredients

1/4 cup bran
1 cup milk
1 cup diabetic applesauce
4tbsp sweetener
1tsp cinnamon

Directions

Blend the ingredients together.

Pour into a heat-proof bowl that fits into your Instant Pot.

Pour a cup of water into the Instant Pot.

Place the bowl in the steamer basket and the basket in the Instant Pot.

Cook on Steam, low pressure, for 20 minutes.

Depressurize quickly and serve.

Nutrition:

Calories: 273 Carbs:
1.5 Sugar: 0 Fat: 27
Protein: 9

Peanut Butter Fudge

Prep Time	Cook Time	Serving
10 Minutes	1 minutes	1

Ingredients

½ cup chocolate chips
4 ounces cream cheese
1/8 cup stevia
2 tablespoons of peanut butter
¼ teaspoon of vanilla extract

Directions

Combine all the ingredients in a mini instant pot and then lock the lid.

Set the timer for one minute at high pressure manually.

Once the cooking is done, allow it to cool.

Stir the mixture by opening the instant pot.

Once mixed well allow it to cook for 25 minutes.

Serve and enjoy.

Nutrition:

Amount per serving Calories1036 % Daily Value* Total Fat 80.6g103% Saturated Fat 45.8g229% Cholesterol 144mg48% Sodium 549mg24% Total Carbohydrate 59.4g22% Dietary Fiber 4.8g17% Total Sugars 46.6g Protein 23g Vitamin D 0mcg0% Calcium 251mg19% Iron 6mg35% Potassium 657mg14%

Cheesecake Bites

Prep Time	Cook Time	Serving
10 Minutes	15 Minutes	1

Ingredients

8 ounces cream cheese, softened
¼ cup powdered stevia
¼ cup peanut flour
1/8 cup sour cream
1 egg, whisked
½ cup Water

Directions

Take a bowl and beat together cream cheese and stevia.

Once the smooth paste is formed, fold in the peanut flour and sour cream.

Mix well and then add whisked egg.

Combine well to form a batter.

Now pour this batter into silicon cupcakes.

Cove the cupcakes with the foil.

Now pour 1/2 cup of water in an instant pot and adjust rack inside the pot.

Place the cupcakes on top of the rack.

Now adjust the cooking timer to 15 minutes.

When the timer beeps, release the steam naturally.

Allow the bites to cool completely.

Once cool off, serve.

Nutrition: *Amount per serving Calories1173 % Daily Value* Total Fat 102.6g132% Saturated Fat 56.8g284% Cholesterol 426mg142% Sodium 752mg33% Total Carbohydrate 26.4g10% Dietary Fiber 9.5g34% Total Sugars 0.8g Protein 43.9g Vitamin D 15mcg77% Calcium 320mg25% Iron 6mg36% Potassium 1186mg25%*

Angel Food Cake

Prep Time	Cook Time	Serving
10 Minutes	40 Minutes	1

Ingredients

½ cup cake flour
Stevia, to taste
Pinch of salt
6 egg whites
½ teaspoon cream of tartar
1 teaspoon Vanilla

Directions

Take a small bowl and combine together cake flour, stevia, and salt.

Take another bowl and whisk egg whites along with vanilla until foamy.

Then add cream of tartar to eggs and mix it well.

Beat it with hand beater until foam peaks the top.

Now add this mixture to the cake flour mixture.

Pour this batter into a small spring form pan. Leave the top space to expand.

Now place a steam rack inside a pot and pour a ¾ cup of water.

Now place the spring pan on top of the rack and close the lid.

Cook for 20 minutes at high pressure. Then manually release the steam.

Remove the lid of the pot and then remove the cake with the oven mitts.

Now, turn the cake upside down and then place in the spring pan.

Now again pour ¾ cup of water to the pot and then adjust the spring pan on top of the rack. Cover and cook about 20 minutes.

After the timer beeps, release the steam by using the quick release Directions.

Take out the pan by opening the lid of the pot. Let it get cool down, then serve.

Nutrition:

Amount per serving
Calories346 % Daily Value* Total Fat 1g1% Saturated Fat 0.1g1% Cholesterol 0mg0% Sodium 357mg16% Total Carbohydrate 50.6g18% Dietary Fiber 1.7g6% Total Sugars 2.1g Protein 28.1g Vitamin D 0mcg0% Calcium 24mg2% Iron 3mg18% Potassium 643mg14%

Apple Crisps

Prep Time	Cook Time	Serving
10 Minutes	7 minutes	2

Ingredients

3 medium sized apples, peeled and chopped into chunks
1/4 teaspoon nutmeg
1/4 cup of water
2 tablespoons butter
3/4 cup old-fashioned rolled oats
1/4 cup of flour
Salt, pinch

Directions

Dump the apple cubes on the bottom of the instant pot.

Now, add nutmeg, and water on top.

Take a small bowl and add butter to it.

Melt the butter in the microwave for 2 minutes.

Then add flour, oat, and salt to the bowl.

Drop this mixture on top of the apple inside the pot.

Now close the pot and secure the lid.

Cook it on high pressure for 7 minutes.

Once done, quick release the steam.

Serve hot or cold.

Enjoy.

Nutrition:

Amount per serving
Calories335 % Daily Value* Total Fat 12.8g16% Saturated Fat 7.6g38% Cholesterol 31mg10% Sodium 161mg7% Total Carbohydrate 54.8g20% Dietary Fiber 9.3g33% Total Sugars 25.5g Protein 3.7g Vitamin D 8mcg40% Calcium 15mg1% Iron 18mg99% Potassium 368mg8%

Chocolate Cake

Prep Time	Cook Time	Serving
10 Minutes	6 Minutes	1

Ingredients

1 egg, whisked
2 tablespoons of Olive Oil
4 tablespoons Milk, Raw
4 tablespoons of All Purpose, Un-bleached
2 tablespoons of sweetened Cacao Powder
Salt, pinch

Directions

Grease the ramekins with oil spray and set aside.

Next, pour a cup of water in your instant pot.

Adjust the trivet inside the instant pot.

Take a bowl and mix all the ingredients in it until finely blended.

Pour this prepared mixture into ramekin dishes.

Fill just slightly below the top.

Place these ramekins inside the Instant Pot on top of the trivet.

Now close the lid and set the timer to 6 minutes.

Once the timer beeps, release the steam and open the pot.

Take out ramekins and let it get cool down.

Then serve.

Nutrition:

Amount per serving
Calories585 % Daily Value* Total Fat 42g54%
Saturated Fat 11.2g56%
Cholesterol 169mg56%
Sodium 246mg11%
Total Carbohydrate 55.1g20% Dietary Fiber 13.1g47% Total Sugars 3.2g Protein 19.8g
Vitamin D 16mcg79%
Calcium 142mg11%
Iron 6mg35% Potassium 139mg3%

Sugar-Free Banana Bread

Prep Time	Cook Time	Serving
10 Minutes	30 Minutes	2

Ingredients

½ cup of butter
2 eggs
3 medium bananas, mashed
1-1/2 cups all-purpose flour
1.5 teaspoons baking soda

Directions

Grease a small Bundt pan with oil spray.

Now line a parchment paper on the bottom of the Bundt pan.

Now pour water about 1/3 cup in the pot and adjust trivet on top.

Now combine eggs along with butter and bananas in a bowl and whisk until smooth.

Then gently fold in flour and baking soda.

Mix to form a batter.

Transfer this batter into Bundt pan.

Place Bundt pan on top of the trivet.

Close the pot and lock the lid.

Cook on high for 30 minutes.

Once done naturally release the steam.

Nutrition:

Amount per serving Calories855 % Daily Value* Total Fat 51.6g66% Saturated Fat 30.8g154% Cholesterol 286mg95% Sodium 1335mg58% Total Carbohydrate 88.5g32% Dietary Fiber 6.3g22% Total Sugars 22.2g Protein 14.4g Vitamin D 47mcg236% Calcium 55mg4% Iron 4mg23% Potassium 773mg16%

Fruitful Compote

Prep Time	Cook Time	Serving
10 Minutes	6 minutes	1

Ingredients

1 cup of blueberries
1 teaspoon cinnamon
2 teaspoons of lemon
1 scoop stevia
Salt, pinch
4 tablespoons of water

Directions

Combine all the listed ingredients in your mini instant pot.

Cook on high pressure for 6 minutes.

Once done, release the steam quickly.

Open the pot and serve the warm compote.

Nutrition:

Amount per serving Calories91 % Daily Value* Total Fat 0.6g1% Saturated Fat 0g0% Cholesterol 0mg0% Sodium 158mg7% Total Carbohydrate 23.7g9% Dietary Fiber 5g18% Total Sugars 14.7g Protein 1.3g Vitamin D 0mcg0% Calcium 28mg2% Iron 2mg12% Potassium 134mg3%

Orange Bites

Prep Time	Cook Time	Serving
10 Minutes	12 Minutes	2

Ingredients

8 ounces Yellow cake mix
1-2 eggs whisked
1 tablespoon butter
3 ounces cream cheese
2 tablespoons orange zest

Directions

Combine cream cheese in a bowl and smooth it out.

Next, add orange zest, egg and butter to the mixture and combine well.

Now fold in the yellow cake mix.

Mix well.

Now pour this in an oil greased small cake pan that fits inside the mini instant pot.

Now place a rack in an instant pot and pour 1/3 cup of water.

Place the cake pan on top of the rack and cover the instant pot.

Cover and cook on high for 12 minutes.

Once done, quick release the steam and open the pot.

Nutrition:

Nutrition: Amount per serving Calories731 % Daily Value* Total Fat 36.2g46% Saturated Fat 15.8g79% Cholesterol 157mg52%
Sodium 947mg41%
Total Carbohydrate 91.4g33% Dietary Fiber 1.9g7% Total Sugars 49.5g Protein 11.5g
Vitamin D 24mcg122%
Calcium 212mg16%
Iron 3mg15% Potassium 193mg4%

Simple and Classic Carrot Cake

Prep Time	Cook Time	Serving
10 Minutes	20 Minutes	1

Ingredients

1-1/2 cups plain flour
Pinch of salt
4-6 tablespoons of butter, unsalted and melted
1 egg, whisked
1 cup almond milk
1 cup carrots, shredded

Directions

Adjust the steamer basket inside the top of the instant pot and pour a generous amount of water about a ½ cup.

Grease a cake pan with oil spray and set aside.

Take a bowl and combine the flour and salt.

In a separate bowl, combine butter, whisked eggs, and milk.

Pour this mixture into the flour mixture.

Fold in shredded carrots.

Mix well to form a batter.

Pour this batter into a cake pan.

Place it on top of the steamer basket.

Select the timer to 20 minutes at high pressure.

Then, allow the steam to release naturally.

Remove the cake from the steamer basket.

Let it get cooled down.

Serve and enjoy.

Nutrition:

Amount per serving Calories1522 % Daily Value* Total Fat 108.9g140% Saturated Fat 81.5g407% Cholesterol 286mg95% Sodium 658mg29% Total Carbohydrate 119.9g44% Dietary Fiber 11.4g41% Total Sugars 14.1g Protein 25.3g Vitamin D 47mcg236% Calcium 130mg10% Iron 11mg60% Potassium 1189mg25%

Chocolate Fondue with Dipper

Prep Time	Cook Time	Serving
10 Minutes	7 minutes	2-3

Ingredients

14 ounces of Dark chocolate
½ cup light cream
2 tablespoons rum
1 cup of whole strawberries

Directions

Pour the chocolate and cream in the mini instant pot

Close the lid, and set the timer to 7 minutes.

Afterward, quick release the steam

Transfer the fondue to a bowl and add rum

Serve with strawberries

Enjoy this simple and sweet treat.

Nutrition:

Amount per serving Calories803 % Daily Value* Total Fat 45.6g58% Saturated Fat 31.4g157% Cholesterol 53mg18% Sodium 112mg5% Total Carbohydrate 82.9g30% Dietary Fiber 5.5g20% Total Sugars 70.5g Protein 10.9g Vitamin D 0mcg0% Calcium 272mg21% Iron 3mg18% Potassium 585mg12%

Banana Bread.

Prep Time	Cook Time	Serving
12 Minutes	55 Minutes	10

Ingredients

3 overripe bananas, peeled, mashed
2 cups self-rising flour
1½ cups sugar
½ cup butter, softened
2 eggs

Directions

Warm the butter until it melts, but do not let it get hot.

Cream the butter, and sugar together. Add the eggs. Stir until fully combined.

Add the flour. Stir well. Add mashed bananas. Stir until a batter forms.

Grease a baking pan that fits the Instant Pot. Pour in the batter.

Let it rest 30 minutes.

Add 1 cup of water to Instant Pot. Place baking pan in the pot.

Seal lid. Cook on Slow for 55 minutes.

Release pressure quickly. Let rest 5 minutes before removing.

Tilt baking pan over, remove banana bread. Allow to cool.

Nutrition:

Total fat: 19.7g Cholesterol: 0mg Sodium: 4mg
Total carbohydrates: 3.6g Dietary fiber: 2.3g
Protein: 1.6g Calcium: 7mg
Potassium: 38mg Iron: 1mg Vitamin D: 0mcg

Pumpkin Spice Oat Bars.

Prep Time	Cook Time	Serving
25 Minutes	10 Minutes	6

Ingredients

1 cup pumpkin puree
1 cup steel-cut oats
¼ cup maple syrup
1 Tbsp soft butter
3 Tbsp pumpkin spice

Directions

Set Instant Pot on high. Melt the butter with open lid.

Add the oats. Toast for 3 minutes.

In a separate bowl, combine the toasted oats, pumpkin puree, maple syrup, and pumpkin spice. Stir well. Grease a loaf pan for Instant Pot.

Seal lid. Cook on Rice for 10 minutes.

Release pressure naturally. Let rest 5 minutes before removing pan.

Allow to cool in pan then cut into bars.

Nutrition:

Total fat: 7.2g Cholesterol: 0mg Sodium: 7mg Total carbohydrates: 5.2g Dietary fiber: 2.4g Protein:0.9g Calcium: 12mg Potassium: 208mg Iron: 0mg Vitamin D: 0mcg

Fruity Rice Pudding.

Prep Time	Cook Time	Serving
15 Minutes	6 minutes	4

Ingredients

3 cups whole milk
1.5 cups Arborio rice
1.5 tsp cinnamon powder
1 cup apple juice
3 cups chopped fresh fruit, your choice

Directions

Add all ingredients to Instant Pot. Stir well.

Seal lid. Cook on Rice setting for 6 minutes.

Release the pressure naturally. Let rest 5 minutes before serving.

Nutrition:

Total fat: 3g Cholesterol: 0mg Sodium: 30mg Total carbohydrates: 2.4g Dietary fiber: 0.9g Protein: 1.2g Calcium: 19mg Potassium: 58mg Iron: 0mg Vitamin D: 0mcg

Tapioca Pudding.

Prep Time	Cook Time	Serving
5 Minutes	10 Minutes	4

Ingredients

1.5 cups water
1¼ cup whole milk
½ cup sugar
⅓ cup tapioca pearls
Zest from ½ lemon

Directions

In a bowl, combine the tapioca, milk, lemon, and sugar. Stir well.

Grease 4 ramekins to fit in Instant Pot. Divide batter between ramekins.

Places ramekins in Instant Pot. Fill water up to halfway mark of ramekins (careful not to cover in water).

Seal lid. Cook on Steam for 10 minutes.

Release the pressure quickly. Let rest 5 minutes before removing.

Nutrition:

Calories: 272 Carbs: 4.4g Protein: 32.1g Fat: 14.2g Sugar: 1.9g

Chia Pudding.

Prep Time	Cook Time	Serving
5 Minutes	5 Minutes	4

Ingredients

2 cups almond milk
½ cup chia seeds
¼ cup coconut, shredded
¼ cup almonds
4 tsp demerara sugar

Directions

Mix the chia seeds, milk, almonds, and coconut in Instant Pot.

Seal lid. Cook on Beans for 5 minutes.

Release pressure quickly. Let rest 5 minutes before serving.

Nutrition:

Calories: 475 Carbs: 1.1g Protein: 35.2g Fat: 36.8g Sugar: 0.5g Sodium: 242mg

---

Coconut Rice.

Prep Time	Cook Time	Serving
7 Minutes	5 minutes	4

Ingredients

1 cup cooked rice
1 cup boiling water
1 cup coconut milk
½ cup coconut chips
Pinch of ground cinnamon

Directions

Combine all the ingredients in Instant Pot.

Seal lid. Cook on Stew for 5 minutes.

Release the pressure quickly. Let rest 5 minutes before serving.

Nutrition:

Calories: 304 Carbs: 1.4g Protein: 26.1g Fat: 21.6g Sugar: 0.1g Sodium: 137mg

Coconut Chia Bowls.

Prep Time	Cook Time	Serving
5 Minutes	5 Minutes	4

Ingredients

2 cups almond milk
½ cup chia seeds
¼ cup candied coconut
¼ cup coconut, shredded
4 tsp demerara sugar

Directions

Mix the chia seeds, milk, almonds, and coconut in Instant Pot.

Seal lid. Cook on Beans for 5 minutes.

Release the pressure quickly. Let rest 5 minutes before serving.

Split between four bowls. Sprinkle demerara sugar on top.

Nutrition:

Calories: 258 Carbs: 2.8g Protein: 24.5g Fat: 16.7g Sugar: 2.7g Sodium: 649mg

Stewed Apples.

Prep Time	Cook Time	Serving
4 Minutes	2 Minutes	4

Ingredients

3 medium apples, peeled, cored, sliced
2 Tbsp water
1 tsp ground cinnamon
1 tsp honey

Directions

Mix all the ingredients together in Instant Pot.

Seal lid. Cook on Stew for 2 minutes.

Release the pressure quickly. Let rest 5 minutes before serving.

Nutrition:

Calories: 335 Carbs: 2.9g Protein: 34g Fat: 20.2g Sugar: 0.8g Sodium: 154mg

---

Fruit And Nut Bake.

Prep Time	Cook Time	Serving
7 Minutes	3 minutes	2

Ingredients

1 cup water
1.5 cups mixed nuts
1 cup mixed berries
1 Tbsp honey
2 tsp butter, melted

Directions

In a food processor or blender, blend the nuts until they look like milled oats.

Pour into a bowl. Add the honey, butter, and water. Stir until fully incorporated.

Pour the mix in the Instant Pot.

Seal lid. Cook on Stew for 3 minutes.

Release pressure quickly. Let rest 5 minutes before serving.

Top with berries.

Nutrition:

Calories: 330 Carbs: 1.5g Protein: 32.6g Fat: 21.5g Sugar: 0.2g Sodium: 458mg

Instant Pot Strawberry Cobbler

Prep Time	Cook Time	Serving
7 Minutes	10 Minutes	4

Ingredients

30 oz strawberries

2½ cups baking mixture

½ cup milk + 3 tbsp melted butter

½ cup granulated white sugar
(divided in 2 parts)

Directions

Make a mixture with strawberries, half portion of white sugar and ½ cup baking mixture. This will make the filling mixture for the cobbler.

Prepare the topping mixture by blending all the other ingredients.

Fill half portions of 4 ramekins with the filling mixture followed by the topping mixture.

Place the steam rack inside the instant pot and then pour a cup of water in the pot. Keep the ramekins in the steam rack and then close the lid of the pot. Use the manual setting and cook on high pressure for 10 minutes. Let the pressure release naturally and then let the dish cool down completely before serving.

Nutrition:

Calories: 258 Carbs: 2.8g Protein: 24.5g Fat: 16.7g Sugar: 2.7g Sodium: 649mg

Buttery Apple Delight

Prep Time	Cook Time	Serving
-	25 Minutes	8

Ingredients

4 large apples, thinly sliced
¼ cup brown sugar
1 tsp cinnamon powder
¼ cup melted butter
Salt, according to taste

Directions

Put all the ingredients in a bowl and toss them thoroughly to coat the apple slices with the other ingredients. Put the coated apple slices in small flat bowls.

Put the steamer rack inside the instant pot and then pour a cup of water. Place the bowls on the rack and then close the lid of the pot. Cook on manual setting for 10 minutes and then let the pressure release naturally.

Let the apples cool down completely before serving.

Wonderful Applesauce from Instant Pot

Prep Time	Cook Time	Serving
-	13 minutes	8

Ingredients

8 apples
1 tsp cinnamon powder
1 cup water
¼ cup melted butter

Directions

Put all the ingredients in the instant pot and cook on manual setting for 8 minutes. Let the pressure release naturally and then remove the lid. Simmer the mixture for few more minutes if you think the mixture is too runny.

Put the entire mixture in a blender and run the device till you have the creamy sauce.

Simplest Bundt Cake

Prep Time	Cook Time	Serving
-	35 Minutes	12

Ingredients

1½ cups all-purpose flour

1½ tsp baking mixture (mixture of baking powder and baking soda)

½ cup mixed dry fruits

½ cup Greek yogurt

¾ cup sugar

Directions

Blend the wet and dry ingredients separately and then mix them together to make the cake batter.

Pour the batter in a greased bundt pan and cover the pan with a foil.

Put the steamer rack inside the instant pot and pour a cup of water. Place the bundt pan on the rack and close the lid. Cook on manual setting for 35 minutes and let the pressure release naturally.

Cool down the cake and then place in the fridge for chilling.

Serve chilled.

Super Easy Instant Pot Pudding

Prep Time	Cook Time	Serving
-	20 Minutes	4

Ingredients

1 cup all-purpose flour + 1 tsp baking powder
½ cup butter
¾ cup brown sugar
2 eggs
½ cup vanilla flavored heavy cream

Directions

Start by mixing butter and sugar in a bowl and then fold in the eggs. Now, fold in the remaining ingredients to prepare the pudding batter.

Pour the batter in a greased pan. Place the pan on the steam rack and pour a cup of water in the pot.

Close the lid and cook on manual setting for 15 minutes. Let the pudding cool down completely before placing inside the fridge. Serve chilled.

Instant Pot Bread Pudding

Prep Time	Cook Time	Serving
-	15 minutes	8

Ingredients

2 cups milk + ¼ cup butter
2 eggs
½ cup sugar
10 slices of cinnamon flavored bread, cubed

Directions

Blend milk, butter, eggs and sugar in a bowl and then soak the bread cubes in this mixture. Put the soaked bread cubes in a baking dish and cover it with a foil.

Place the steam rack inside the instant pot and pour a cup of water. Place the rack in the pot and cover the lid. Cook on manual setting for 15 minutes and then let the pressure release naturally.

Serve after cooling down completely or you can serve the pudding chilled.

Majestic Peach Sauce

Prep Time	Cook Time	Serving
-	13 Minutes	8

Ingredients

Ingredients:
8 peaches, chopped
1 tsp cardamom powder
1 cup water
¼ cup melted butter

Directions

Put all the ingredients in the instant pot and cook on manual setting for 8 minutes. Let the pressure release naturally and then remove the lid. Simmer the mixture for few more minutes if you think the mixture is too runny.

Put the entire mixture in a blender and run the device till you have the creamy sauce.

Sauce-de-Mango

Prep Time	Cook Time	Serving
-	13 Minutes	8

Ingredients

5 cups ripe mango cubes
1 tsp clove powder
1 cup water
¼ cup melted butter

Directions

Put all the ingredients in the instant pot and cook on manual setting for 8 minutes. Let the pressure release naturally and then remove the lid. Simmer the mixture for few more minutes if you think the mixture is too runny.

Put the entire mixture in a blender and run the device till you have the creamy sauce

Summer Special Mango & Bread Pudding

Prep Time	Cook Time	Serving
-	15 minutes	8

Ingredients

2 cups milk + ¼ cup butter
2 eggs
½ cup sugar
½ cup mango pulp
10 slices of bread, cubed

Directions

Blend milk, mango pulp, butter, eggs and sugar in a bowl and then soak the bread cubes in this mixture. Put the soaked bread cubes in a baking dish and cover it with a foil.

Place the steam rack inside the instant pot and pour a cup of water. Place the rack in the pot and cover the lid. Cook on manual setting for 15 minutes and then let the pressure release naturally.

Serve after cooling down completely or you can serve the pudding chilled.

Strawberry Delight Bread Pudding

Prep Time	Cook Time	Serving
-	13 Minutes	8

Ingredients

2 cups milk + ¼ cup butter

2 eggs

½ cup mashed strawberries

½ cup sugar

10 slices of bread, cubed

Directions

Blend milk, mashed strawberries, butter, eggs and sugar in a bowl and then soak the bread cubes in this mixture. Put the soaked bread cubes in a baking dish and cover it with a foil.

Place the steam rack inside the instant pot and pour a cup of water. Place the rack in the pot and cover the lid. Cook on manual setting for 15 minutes and then let the pressure release naturally.

Serve after cooling down completely or you can serve the pudding chilled.

Magical Orange Flavored Pudding

Prep Time	Cook Time	Serving
-	15 Minutes	8

Ingredients

2 cups milk + ¼ cup butter
2 eggs
½ cup orange pulp
½ cup sugar
10 slices of bread, cubed

Directions

Blend milk, butter, orange pulp, eggs and sugar in a bowl and then soak the bread cubes in this mixture. Put the soaked bread cubes in a baking dish and cover it with a foil.

Place the steam rack inside the instant pot and pour a cup of water. Place the rack in the pot and cover the lid. Cook on manual setting for 15 minutes and then let the pressure release naturally.

Serve after cooling down completely or you can serve the pudding chilled.

Superlicious Lemon Sauce

Prep Time	Cook Time	Serving
-	13 minutes	8

Ingredients

1 cup lemon pulp
1 tsp cinnamon powder
½ cup granulated white sugar
1 cup water
¼ cup melted butter

Directions

Put all the ingredients in the instant pot and cook on manual setting for 8 minutes. Let the pressure release naturally and then remove the lid. Simmer the mixture for few more minutes if you think the mixture is too runny.

Put the entire mixture in a blender and run the device till you have the creamy sauce.

Tangy Orange Sauce

Prep Time	Cook Time	Serving
-	13 Minutes	8

Ingredients

2 cups orange pulp

1 tsp cinnamon powder

½ cup granulated sugar

1 cup water

¼ cup melted butter

Directions

Put all the ingredients in the instant pot and cook on manual setting for 8 minutes. Let the pressure release naturally and then remove the lid. Simmer the mixture for few more minutes if you think the mixture is too runny.

Put the entire mixture in a blender and run the device till you have the creamy sauce.

Super Nutty Cobbler

Prep Time	Cook Time	Serving
-	10 Minutes	4

Ingredients

30 oz shredded coconut
2½ cups baking mixture
½ cup milk + 3 tbsp melted butter
½ cup granulated white sugar (divided in 2 parts)
½ cup chopped walnuts

Directions

Make a mixture with coconut, half portion of white sugar and ½ cup baking mixture. This will make the filling mixture for the cobbler.

Prepare the topping mixture by blending all the other ingredients.

Fill half portions of 4 ramekins with the filling mixture followed by the topping mixture.

Place the steam rack inside the instant pot and then pour a cup of water in the pot. Keep the ramekins in the steam rack and then close the lid of the pot. Use the manual setting and cook on high pressure for 10 minutes. Let the pressure release naturally and then let the dish cool down completely before serving..

Orange Magic Cobbler

Prep Time	Cook Time	Serving
-	10 minutes	4

Ingredients

30 oz orange pulp
Zest of ½ orange
2½ cups baking mixture
½ cup milk + 3 tbsp melted butter
½ cup granulated white sugar (divided in 2 parts)

Directions

Make a mixture with orange zest and pulp, half portion of white sugar and ½ cup baking mixture. This will make the filling mixture for the cobbler.

Prepare the topping mixture by blending all the other ingredients.

Fill half portions of 4 ramekins with the filling mixture followed by the topping mixture.

Place the steam rack inside the instant pot and then pour a cup of water in the pot. Keep the ramekins in the steam rack and then close the lid of the pot. Use the manual setting and cook on high pressure for 10 minutes. Let the pressure release naturally and then let the dish cool down completely before serving.

Mango Cobbler Magic

Prep Time	Cook Time	Serving
-	10 Minutes	4

Ingredients

2 cups mango pulp

2½ cups baking mixture

½ cup milk + 3 tbsp melted butter

½ cup granulated white sugar
(divided in 2 parts)

Directions

Make a mixture with mango, half portion of white sugar and ½ cup baking mixture. This will make the filling mixture for the cobbler.

Prepare the topping mixture by blending all the other ingredients.

Fill half portions of 4 ramekins with the filling mixture followed by the topping mixture.

Place the steam rack inside the instant pot and then pour a cup of water in the pot. Keep the ramekins in the steam rack and then close the lid of the pot. Use the manual setting and cook on high pressure for 10 minutes. Let the pressure release naturally and then let the dish cool down completely before serving.

Preaching Peach Cobbler

Prep Time	Cook Time	Serving
-	10 Minutes	4

Ingredients

2 cups peach pulp
2½ cups baking mixture
½ cup milk + 3 tbsp melted butter
½ cup granulated white sugar
(divided in 2 parts)

Directions

Make a mixture with peach, half portion of white sugar and ½ cup baking mixture. This will make the filling mixture for the cobbler.

Prepare the topping mixture by blending all the other ingredients.

Fill half portions of 4 ramekins with the filling mixture followed by the topping mixture.

Place the steam rack inside the instant pot and then pour a cup of water in the pot. Keep the ramekins in the steam rack and then close the lid of the pot. Use the manual setting and cook on high pressure for 10 minutes. Let the pressure release naturally and then let the dish cool down completely before serving.

Utterly Butterly Sliced Peach

Prep Time	Cook Time	Serving
-	25 minutes	8

Ingredients

4 large peaches, thinly sliced
¼ cup brown sugar
1 tsp cinnamon powder
¼ cup melted butter
Salt, according to taste

Directions

Put all the ingredients in a bowl and toss them thoroughly to coat the peach slices with the other ingredients. Put the coated peach slices in small flat bowls.

Put the steamer rack inside the instant pot and then pour a cup of water. Place the bowls on the rack and then close the lid of the pot. Cook on manual setting for 10 minutes and then let the pressure release naturally.

Let the peach slices cool down completely before serving.

Sweet Pumpkin Slices for Dessert

Prep Time	Cook Time	Serving
-	10 Minutes	4

Ingredients

1 large bowl pumpkin slices
¼ cup brown sugar
1 tsp cinnamon powder
¼ cup melted butter
Salt, according to taste

Directions

Put all the ingredients in a bowl and toss them thoroughly to coat the pumpkin slices with the other ingredients. Put the coated pumpkin slices in small flat bowls.

Put the steamer rack inside the instant pot and then pour a cup of water. Place the bowls on the rack and then close the lid of the pot. Cook on manual setting for 10 minutes and then let the pressure release naturally.

Let the pumpkin slices cool down completely before serving.

Lightning Lichi Sauce

Prep Time	Cook Time	Serving
-	13 Minutes	8

Ingredients

2 cups lichi pulp
1 tsp cinnamon powder
½ cup granulated sugar
1 cup water
¼ cup melted butter

Directions

Put all the ingredients in the instant pot and cook on manual setting for 8 minutes. Let the pressure release naturally and then remove the lid. Simmer the mixture for few more minutes if you think the mixture is too runny.

Put the entire mixture in a blender and run the device till you have the creamy sauce.

Strawberry Delight Bundt Cake

Prep Time	Cook Time	Serving
-	35minutes	12

Ingredients

1½ cups all-purpose flour
1½ tsp baking mixture (mixture of baking powder and baking soda)
½ cup frozen strawberries
½ cup Greek yogurt
¾ cup sugar

Directions

Blend the wet and dry ingredients separately and then mix them together to make the cake batter.

Pour the batter in a greased bundt pan and cover the pan with a foil.

Put the steamer rack inside the instant pot and pour a cup of water. Place the bundt pan on the rack and close the lid. Cook on manual setting for 35 minutes and let the pressure release naturally.

Cool down the cake and then place in the fridge for chilling.

Serve chilled.

Mango Magic Bundt Cake

Prep Time	Cook Time	Serving
-	35 Minutes	12

Ingredients

1½ cups all-purpose flour
1½ tsp baking mixture (mixture of baking powder and baking soda)
1 cup cubed ripe mango
½ cup Greek yogurt
¾ cup sugar

Directions

Blend the wet and dry ingredients separately and then mix them together to make the cake batter.

Pour the batter in a greased bundt pan and cover the pan with a foil.

Put the steamer rack inside the instant pot and pour a cup of water. Place the bundt pan on the rack and close the lid. Cook on manual setting for 35 minutes and let the pressure release naturally.

Cool down the cake and then place in the fridge for chilling.

Serve chilled.

Strange Orange Bundt Slices

Prep Time	Cook Time	Serving
-	35 Minutes	12

Ingredients

1½ cups all-purpose flour
1½ tsp baking mixture (mixture of baking powder and baking soda)
1 cup dried oranges, chopped
½ cup Greek yogurt
¾ cup sugar

Directions

Blend the wet and dry ingredients separately and then mix them together to make the cake batter.

Pour the batter in a greased bundt pan and cover the pan with a foil.

Put the steamer rack inside the instant pot and pour a cup of water. Place the bundt pan on the rack and close the lid. Cook on manual setting for 35 minutes and let the pressure release naturally.

Cool down the cake and then place in the fridge for chilling.

Slice the bundt cake into desired sizes and then serve.

Main Dish Recipes

Butternut And Chard Soup

Prep Time	Cook Time	Serving
10 Minutes	20 Minutes	6

Ingredients

1 tablespoon olive oil
1 yellow onion, chopped
3 big carrots, chopped
3 celery stalks, chopped
4 thyme sprigs
8 cups chicken stock
A pinch of salt and pepper
1 teaspoon rosemary, chopped
4 cups Swiss chard leaves, chopped
2 cups butternut squash, peeled and cubed
4 garlic cloves, minced
1 cup coconut cream

Directions

1. Set your instant pot on sauté mode, add the oil, heat it up, add carrots, onion and celery, stir and sauté for a couple of minutes.

2. Add thyme spring, chicken stock, salt, pepper, butternut squash, garlic and rosemary, stir, cover and cook on High for 18 minutes.

3. Discard thyme, add Swiss chard and coconut cream, stir, set on sauté mode for a couple more minutes, ladle into bowls and serve.

Enjoy!

Nutrition:

calories 210, fat 3, fiber 1, carbs 5, protein 8

Tender Pork Chops

Prep Time	Cook Time	Serving
10 Minutes	20 minutes	4

Ingredients

4 pork chops, boneless
1 cup water
2 tablespoons olive oil
10 ounces Paleo cream of mushroom soup
1 cup coconut cream
A pinch of sea salt and black pepper
A handful parsley, chopped

Directions

1. Set your instant pot on Sauté mode, add oil, heat it up, add pork chops, salt and pepper and brown them for a few minutes.

2. Add water, stir, cover and cook on High for 10 minutes.

3. Transfer pork chops to a platter and leave aside.

4. Set the pot on Simmer mode, heat up the cooking liquid, add mushroom soup, stir, cook for 2 minutes and take off heat.

5. Add parsley and coconut cream and stir.

6. Divide pork chops on plates, drizzle the sauce all over and serve.

Enjoy!

Nutrition:

calories 244 , fat 8 , fiber 1, carbs 7, protein 22

Asian Style Salmon

Prep Time	Cook Time	Serving
10 Minutes	10 Minutes	2

Ingredients

2 salmon fillets, boneless

1 cup water

A pinch of sea salt and black pepper

2 tablespoons coconut aminos

2 tablespoons maple syrup

16 ounces broccoli and cauliflower florets

2 tablespoons lemon juice

1 teaspoon sesame seeds

Directions

1. Put the cauliflower, broccoli florets and salmon in a heat proof dish.

2. In a bowl, mix maple syrup with aminos and lemon juice and whisk well.

3. Pour this over salmon and veggies, season with black pepper to the taste and sprinkle sesame seeds on top.

4. Put the water in your instant pot, add the steamer basket, add the dish with the salmon and veggies, cover and cook on High for 4 minutes.

5. Divide everything between plates and serve.

Enjoy!

Nutrition: *calories 180, fat 4, fiber 2, carbs 6, protein 5*

Creamy Soup

Prep Time	Cook Time	Serving
6 Minutes	15 Minutes	8

Ingredients

6 bacon slices, cooked and chopped
1 pound chicken sausage, ground and cooked
1 tablespoon ghee, melted
1 cup yellow onion, chopped
2 garlic cloves, minced
14 ounces chicken stock
A pinch of sea salt and black pepper
A pinch of red pepper flakes
3 sweet potatoes, chopped
2 tablespoons arrowroot powder
12 ounces coconut milk
2 cups spinach, chopped

Directions

1. Put the ghee, onion, garlic, stock, salt, pepper, red pepper flakes and sausage in your instant pot, stir, cover and cook on High for 10 minutes.

2. In a bowl, mix arrowroot powder with coconut milk, whisk and add to the soup.

3. Add spinach, stir, cover and cook on High for 3 minutes more.

4. Add bacon, stir, ladle into bowls and serve.

Enjoy!

Nutrition:

calories 184, fat 3, fiber 3, carbs 6, protein 8

Easy Tomato Soup

Prep Time	Cook Time	Serving
10 Minutes	15 minutes	4

Ingredients

35 oz tomatoes, chopped
1 yellow onion, chopped
2 garlic cloves, minced
1 tablespoon olive oil
2 teaspoons thyme, chopped
1 tablespoon ghee, melted
1 cup veggie stock
½ cup coconut cream
A pinch of sea salt and black pepper

Directions

1. Set your instant pot on Sauté mode, add the oil and the ghee and heat up.

2. Add onion and garlic, stir and sauté for 3 minutes.

3. Add tomatoes, thyme, stock, salt and pepper, stir, cover and cook on High for 12 minutes.

4. Add cream, stir, ladle into bowls and serve.

Enjoy!

Nutrition:

calories 200, fat 1, fiber 3, carbs 5, protein 7

Carrot And Ginger Soup

Prep Time	Cook Time	Serving
10 Minutes	20 Minutes	4

Ingredients

2 and ½ pounds carrots, chopped

2 tablespoons ginger, grated

2 tablespoons olive oil

2 garlic cloves, minced

1 cup yellow onion, chopped

4 cups veggie stock

4 ounces coconut milk

1 cup water

3 tablespoons ghee, melted

Salt and pepper to the taste

Directions

1. Put carrots, ginger, olive oil, onion, garlic, veggie stock, water, milk, ghee, salt and pepper in your instant pot, stir, cover and cook on High for 20 minutes.

2. Blend soup using an immersion blender, stir, ladle into bowls and serve.

Enjoy!

Nutrition: *calories 178, fat 4, fiber 2, carbs 3, protein 5*

Creamy Soup

Prep Time	Cook Time	Serving
6 Minutes	15 Minutes	8

Ingredients

6 bacon slices, cooked and chopped
1 pound chicken sausage, ground and cooked
1 tablespoon ghee, melted
1 cup yellow onion, chopped
2 garlic cloves, minced
14 ounces chicken stock
A pinch of sea salt and black pepper
A pinch of red pepper flakes
3 sweet potatoes, chopped
2 tablespoons arrowroot powder
12 ounces coconut milk
2 cups spinach, chopped

Directions

1. Put the ghee, onion, garlic, stock, salt, pepper, red pepper flakes and sausage in your instant pot, stir, cover and cook on High for 10 minutes.

2. In a bowl, mix arrowroot powder with coconut milk, whisk and add to the soup.

3. Add spinach, stir, cover and cook on High for 3 minutes more.

4. Add bacon, stir, ladle into bowls and serve.

Enjoy!

Nutrition:

calories 184, fat 3, fiber 3, carbs 6, protein 8

Easy Tomato Soup

Prep Time	Cook Time	Serving
10 Minutes	15 minutes	4

Ingredients

35 oz tomatoes, chopped
1 yellow onion, chopped
2 garlic cloves, minced
1 tablespoon olive oil
2 teaspoons thyme, chopped
1 tablespoon ghee, melted
1 cup veggie stock
½ cup coconut cream
A pinch of sea salt and black pepper

Directions

1. Set your instant pot on Sauté mode, add the oil and the ghee and heat up.

2. Add onion and garlic, stir and sauté for 3 minutes.

3. Add tomatoes, thyme, stock, salt and pepper, stir, cover and cook on High for 12 minutes.

4. Add cream, stir, ladle into bowls and serve.

Enjoy!

Nutrition:

calories 200, fat 1, fiber 3, carbs 5, protein 7

Carrot And Ginger Soup

Prep Time	Cook Time	Serving
10 Minutes	20 Minutes	4

Ingredients

2 and ½ pounds carrots, chopped

2 tablespoons ginger, grated

2 tablespoons olive oil

2 garlic cloves, minced

1 cup yellow onion, chopped

4 cups veggie stock

4 ounces coconut milk

1 cup water

3 tablespoons ghee, melted

Salt and pepper to the taste

Directions

1. Put carrots, ginger, olive oil, onion, garlic, veggie stock, water, milk, ghee, salt and pepper in your instant pot, stir, cover and cook on High for 20 minutes.

2. Blend soup using an immersion blender, stir, ladle into bowls and serve.

Enjoy!

Nutrition: *calories 178, fat 4, fiber 2, carbs 3, protein 5*

Red Peppers Soup

Prep Time	Cook Time	Serving
5 Minutes	15 Minutes	4

Ingredients

6 red bell peppers, sliced

2 red onions, chopped

2 garlic cloves, minced

4 plum tomatoes, sliced

1 sweet potato, chopped

6 cups chicken stock

2 tablespoons olive oil

A pinch of sea salt and black pepper

Directions

1. Set your instant pot on Sauté mode, add the oil and heat it up.

2. Add red peppers, garlic and onion, stir and sauté for 3 minutes

1. Add tomatoes, chicken stock and sweet potato, stir, cover and cook on High for 13 minutes more.

2. Add a pinch of salt and black pepper, stir, ladle into bowls and serve.

Enjoy!

Nutrition:

calories 193, fat 3, fiber 1, carbs 5, protein 7

Delicious Fish Stew

Prep Time	Cook Time	Serving
10 Minutes	10 minutes	8

Ingredients

14 ounces chicken stock

4 sweet potatoes, cubed

3 carrots, chopped

1 yellow onion, chopped

2 garlic cloves, minced

¼ cup parsley, chopped

1 bay leaf

¼ teaspoon saffron powder

1 pound halibut, boneless and cubed

1 red bell pepper, chopped

Directions

1. Put the chicken stock in your instant pot, add sweet potatoes, carrots, onion, garlic, saffron, parsley and bay leaf, stir, cover and cook on High for 4 minutes

2. Add fish and red bell pepper, cover and cook on High for 6 minutes more.

3. Discard bay leaf, divide fish stew between plates and serve.

Enjoy!

Nutrition:

calories 200, fat 3, fiber 1, carbs 5, protein 6

Chicken Stew

Prep Time	Cook Time	Serving
10 Minutes	20 Minutes	4

Ingredients

3 sweet potatoes, cubed

1 yellow onion, cut into medium chunks

1 whole chicken, cut into 8 pieces

2 bay leaves

1 cup water

4 tomatoes, cut into medium chunks

A pinch of sea salt and pepper

Directions

1. Put chicken pieces in your instant pot, add sweet potatoes, onions, tomatoes, bay leaves, water, salt and pepper, stir, cover and cook on High for 20 minutes.

2. Divide among plates and serve hot.

Enjoy!

Nutrition: *calories 200, fat 2, fiber 1, carbs 5, protein 8*

Veggie Stew

Prep Time	Cook Time	Serving
10 Minutes	12 Minutes	4

Ingredients

1 eggplant, chopped
1 zucchini, chopped
1 yellow squash, peeled and cubed
1 red bell pepper, chopped
1 and ½ cups tomatoes, chopped
1 yellow onion, chopped
1 bay leaf
1 cup water
3 garlic cloves, minced
3 tablespoons olive oil
2 tablespoons thyme, chopped
2 tablespoons parsley, chopped
½ cup basil, chopped
A pinch of salt and black pepper

Directions

1. Set your instant pot on Sauté mode, add oil and heat it up.

2. Add onion, garlic, eggplant, zucchini, yellow squash, bell pepper, tomatoes and bay leaf, stir and sauté for a couple of minutes.

3. Add thyme, basil, parsley, salt, pepper and the water, stir, cover and cook on High for 10 minutes.

4. Divide among plates and serve hot.

Enjoy!

Nutrition:

calories 219, fat 2, fiber 2, carbs 6, protein 10

Special Pork And Sauce

Prep Time	Cook Time	Serving
10 Minutes	1 hour	4

Ingredients

1 and ½ pounds pork shoulder, cubed
3 garlic cloves, minced
1 yellow onion, chopped
1 cinnamon stick
Juice from 1 orange
½ cup water
A pinch of sea salt and black pepper
1 tablespoon ginger, grated
2 whole cloves
1 teaspoon rosemary, dried
1 tablespoon maple syrup
2 tablespoons coconut aminos
1 tablespoon olive oil
1 tablespoon honey
1 and ½ tablespoons arrowroot powder

Directions

1. Set your instant pot on Sauté mode, add the oil, heat it up, add pork, salt and pepper, brown for 5 minutes on each side and transfer to a plate.

2. Add onions, ginger, salt and pepper to the pot, stir and sauté them for 1 minute.

3. Add garlic and sauté for 1 minute more.

4. Add orange juice, water, aminos, honey, maple syrup, cinnamon, cloves, rosemary and return pork, stir, cover and cook on High for 50 minutes.

5. Discard cinnamon and cloves, add arrowroot powder, stir well, set pot on Sauté mode and cook until it thickens.

6. Divide everything between plates and serve.

Enjoy!

Nutrition:

calories 240 , fat 6, fiber 1, carbs 6, protein 16

Beef Stew

Prep Time	Cook Time	Serving
10 Minutes	25 Minutes	6

Ingredients

1 tablespoon olive oil

2 pound beef chuck, cubed

1 teaspoon rosemary, chopped

1 yellow onion, chopped

2 carrots, chopped

1 ounce porcini mushrooms, chopped

1 celery stalk, chopped

1 and ½ cups beef stock

A pinch of salt and black pepper

2 tablespoons coconut flour

2 tablespoons ghee, melted

Directions

1. Set your instant pot on Sauté mode, add oil and beef, stir, brown for 5 minutes and mix with onion, celery, rosemary, salt, pepper, carrots, mushrooms and stock.

2. Cover pot, cook on High for 15 minutes and then transfer to Simmer mode.

3. Heat up a pan with the ghee over medium high heat, add flour and 6 tablespoons cooking liquid from the stew, stir and pour over beef stew.

4. Simmer for 5 minutes, divide into bowls and serve.

Enjoy!

Nutrition: *calories 261, fat 4, fiber 3, carbs 8, protein 18*

Cold Veggie Delight

Prep Time	Cook Time	Serving
10 Minutes	10 Minutes	4

Ingredients

½ cup olive oil
1 yellow onion, finely chopped
3 tomatoes, chopped
1 garlic clove, minced
¼ cup parsley, chopped
¼ cup dill, chopped
1 teaspoon basil, chopped
1 cup veggie stock
3 sweet potatoes, chopped
2 zucchinis, chopped
2 carrots, chopped
3 celery stalks, chopped
1 green bell pepper, thinly sliced
Salt and black pepper to the taste

Directions

1. Set your instant pot on sauté mode, add the oil, heat it up, add onion, stir and cook for 2 minutes.

2. Add parsley, garlic and dill, stir and sauté for 1 minute more.

1. Add stock, basil, tomatoes, zucchinis, sweet potatoes, carrots, green bell pepper, celery, salt and pepper, stir, cover and cook on High for 6 minutes.

2. Divide among plates and serve cold

Enjoy!

Nutrition:

calories 140, fat 5, fiber 2, carbs 3, protein 8

Mushroom Stew

Prep Time	Cook Time	Serving
10 Minutes	15 minutes	4

Ingredients

8 ounces shiitake mushrooms, roughly chopped
4 ounces white mushrooms, roughly chopped
1 tablespoon ginger, grated
1 and ¼ cups veggie stock
½ cup red onion, finely chopped
½ cup celery, chopped
½ cup carrot, chopped
5 garlic cloves, minced
Salt and black pepper to the taste
¼ teaspoon oregano, dry
28 ounces canned tomatoes, chopped
1 and ½ teaspoons turmeric powder
¼ cup basil leaves, chopped

Directions

1. Set your instant pot on sauté mode, add ¼ cup stock and heat it up.

2. Add mushrooms, onion, celery, carrot, ginger and garlic, stir and sauté for 5 minutes.

3. Add the rest of the stock, tomatoes, salt, pepper, turmeric and oregano, stir, cover and cook on High for 10 minutes.

4. Add basil, divide among plates and serve right away.

Enjoy!

Nutritio

Nutrition:

calories 70, fat 3, fiber 1, carbs 5, protein 3

Different And Special Stew

Prep Time	Cook Time	Serving
10 Minutes	25 Minutes	4

Ingredients

1 pound beef, cubed

2 bacon slices, cooked and crumbled

2 tablespoons olive oil

½ cup coconut flour

2 cups beef stock

A pinch of sea salt and black pepper

1 cup pearl onions, peeled

4 carrots, chopped

4 garlic cloves, minced

1 tablespoon tomato paste

½ cup water

A small bunch thyme, chopped

A small bunch rosemary, chopped

2 bay leaves

Directions

1. In a bowl, mix coconut flour with a pinch of salt and pepper, dredge beef cubes in this mix and place them on a plate

2. Set your instant pot on Sauté mode, add oil, heat up, add meat, brown on all sides and transfer to a clean plate.

3. Add garlic, water, stock, thyme, carrots, tomato paste, rosemary and onions, stir and sauté for a couple of minutes.

4. Return beef to pot, add bay leaves and bacon, cover and cook at High for 20 minutes

5. Discard bay leaves, divide into bowls and serve right away.

Enjoy!

Nutrition: *calories 298, fat 4, fiber 6, carbs 9, protein 18*

Mexican Chicken Soup

Prep Time	Cook Time	Serving
10 Minutes	17 Minutes	4

Ingredients

4 chicken breasts, skinless and boneless
2 tablespoons olive oil
16 ounces Paleo salsa
1 yellow onion, chopped
3 garlic cloves, minced
29 ounces canned tomatoes, peeled and chopped
29 ounces chicken stock
A pinch of sea salt and black pepper
2 tablespoons parsley, chopped
1 teaspoon garlic powder
1 tablespoon onion powder
1 tablespoon chili powder

Directions

1. Set your instant pot on Sauté mode, add oil, heat it up, add onion and garlic, stir and sauté for 5 minutes.

2. Add chicken breasts, salsa, tomatoes, stock, salt, pepper, parsley, garlic powder, onion and chili powder, stir, cover and cook at High for 8 minutes.

3. Transfer chicken breasts to a cutting board, shred, return to pot, stir, and set the pot on Simmer mode, cook soup for 3 minutes more, ladle into bowls and serve.

Enjoy!

Nutrition:

calories 210, fat 3, fiber 4, carbs 7, protein 14

Creamy Carrot Soup

Prep Time	Cook Time	Serving
10 Minutes	15 minutes	4

Ingredients

1 tablespoon olive oil
1 yellow onion, chopped
1 tablespoon ghee
1 garlic clove, minced
1 pound carrots, chopped
1 inch ginger piece, grated
A pinch of sea salt and black pepper
¼ teaspoon stevia
2 cups chicken stock
14 ounces canned coconut milk
A handful cilantro, chopped

Directions

1. Set your instant pot on Sauté mode, add ghee and oil, heat up, add onion, garlic and ginger, stir and sauté for 4 minutes.

2. Add carrots, stevia, salt and pepper, stir and cook 2 minutes more.

3. Add coconut milk and stock, stir, cover and cook at High for 6 minutes.

4. Blend soup using an immersion blender, add cilantro, stir gently, ladle into bowls and serve.

Enjoy!

Nutrition:

calories 84, fat 2, fiber 3, carbs 8, protein 9

Cauliflower Soup

Prep Time	Cook Time	Serving
10 Minutes	30 Minutes	8

Ingredients

½ teaspoon cumin seeds

1 tablespoon ginger, grated

3 garlic cloves, minced

1 yellow onion, chopped

1 chili pepper, minced

A pinch of cinnamon powder

4 cups veggie stock

3 cups water

1 pound sweet potatoes, peeled and cubed

1 tablespoon curry powder

1 cauliflower head, florets separated

15 ounces canned tomatoes, chopped

A pinch of sea salt and cayenne pepper

1 tablespoon cashew butter

Directions

1. Set your instant pot on sauté mode, add onions, stir and brown for a couple of minutes.

2. Add ginger, cumin seeds, chili and garlic, stir and cook 1 minute more.

3. Add potatoes, stock, curry powder and cinnamon, stir, cover and cook on High for 16 minutes.

4. Add tomatoes, cauliflower, the water, salt and cayenne, stir, cover and cook on High for 10 more minutes.

5. Add cashews butter, stir, ladle into bowls and serve hot.

Enjoy!

Nutrition: calories 113, fat 1, fiber 3, carbs 6, protein 6

Cod Fillets And Orange Sauce

Prep Time	Cook Time	Serving
10 Minutes	10 Minutes	4

Ingredients

4 spring onions, chopped
1 inch ginger piece, grated
1 tablespoon olive oil
4 cod fillets, boneless and skinless
Juice from 1 orange
Zest from 1 orange, grated
A pinch of salt and black pepper
1 cup veggie stock

Directions

1. Season cod with salt and pepper, rub them with oil and leave aside for now.

2. Put ginger, orange juice, orange zest, onions and stock in your instant pot, add the steamer basket, place the fish inside, cover the pot and cook on High for 10 minutes.

3. Divide fish on plates, top with the orange sauce from the pot and serve right away.

Enjoy!

Nutrition:

calories 187, fat 3, fiber 2, carbs 4, protein 6

Special Cod Dish

Prep Time	Cook Time	Serving
5 Minutes	10 minutes	4

Ingredients

1 garlic clove, minced
1 tablespoon olive oil
1 cup water
17 ounces cherry tomatoes, halved
4 cod fillets, boneless and skinless
2 tablespoons capers, chopped
1 cup black olives, pitted and chopped
A pinch of sea salt and black pepper
1 tablespoon parsley, finely chopped

Directions

1. In a heat proof dish, mix tomatoes with salt, pepper, parsley, oil, fish, olives, capers and garlic and toss to coat.

2. Put the water in your instant pot, add the steamer basket, place the dish inside, cover and cook on High for 8 minutes.

3. Divide fish mix between plates and serve.

Enjoy!

Nutrition:

calories 187, fat 3, fiber 3, carbs 6, protein 7

Light Salmon

Prep Time	Cook Time	Serving
5 Minutes	5 Minutes	4

Ingredients

*4 medium salmon fillets, boneless
and skin on*
1 bay leaf
1 teaspoon fennel seeds
4 scallions, chopped
Zest from 1 lemon, grated
1 teaspoon balsamic vinegar
3 peppercorns
¼ cup dill, chopped
2 cups chicken stock
A pinch of sea salt and black pepper

Directions

1. In your instant pot, mix scallions with stock, peppercorns, lemon zest, vinegar, fennel, wine, dill and bay leaf, stir, add the steamer basket and place salmon fillets inside.

2. Season with a pinch of salt and pepper, cover and cook on High for 5 minutes.

3. Divide fish fillets between plates and leave them aside.

4. Set the pot on Simmer more, cook the sauce for a couple more minutes, drizzle over salmon and serve right away.

Enjoy!

Nutrition: *calories 187, fat 3, fiber 3, carbs 6, protein 7*

Wonderful Salmon And Veggies

Prep Time	Cook Time	Serving
10 Minutes	10 Minutes	2

Ingredients

1 cinnamon stick
1 tablespoon olive oil
1 cup water
2 salmon fillets, boneless and skin on
1 bay leaf
3 cloves
2 cups broccoli florets
1 cup baby carrots
A pinch of sea salt and black pepper
Some lime wedges for serving

Directions

1. Put the water in your instant pot and add cinnamon, cloves and bay leaf.

2. Add the steamer basket, place salmon inside, season with salt and pepper, brush it with the oil and mix with carrots and broccoli.

3. Cover instant pot and cook on High for 6 minutes.

4. Divide salmon and veggies on plates, discard bay leaf, cloves and cinnamon, drizzle the sauce from the pot and serve with lime wedges on the side.

Enjoy!

Nutrition:

calories 172, fat 3, fiber 1, carbs 2, protein 3

White Fish Delight

Prep Time	Cook Time	Serving
5 Minutes	25 minutes	6

Ingredients

1 yellow onion, chopped
6 white fish fillets, cut into medium cubes
A pinch of salt and black pepper
13 ounces sweet potatoes, peeled and cubed
13 ounces coconut milk
14 ounces chicken stock
14 ounces coconut cream
14 ounces water

Directions

1. Put potatoes, fish, onion, milk, stock and water in your instant pot, stir, cover and cook on High for 10 minutes

2. Set your instant pot on Simmer more, add coconut cream, salt and pepper, stir and cook for 10 minutes more.

3. Divide this into serving bowls and serve.

Enjoy!

Nutrition:

calories 254, fat 3, fiber 2, carbs 5, protein 12

Healthy Mackerel

Prep Time	Cook Time	Serving
10 Minutes	6 Minutes	4

Ingredients

8 shallots, chopped

1 teaspoon shrimp powder

3 garlic cloves, minced

18 ounces mackerel, boneless and chopped

1 teaspoon turmeric powder

2 lemongrass sticks, halved

1 tablespoon chili paste

1 inch ginger, grated

4 ounces water

5 tablespoons olive oil

6 laska leaves stalks

1 tablespoon stevia

A pinch of salt

Directions

1. In a food processor, mix chili paste with shrimp powder, shallots and turmeric and blend well.

2. Set your instant pot on Sauté mode, add the oil, heat it up, add the paste you've made, mackerel,, lemon grass, laska leaves, ginger, salt and stevia, stir and sauté for 1 minute.

3. Add water, stir, cover and cook on High for 5 minutes

4. Divide fish mix between plates and serve.

Enjoy!

Nutrition: *calories 212, fat 2, fiber 1, carbs 3, protein 7*

Fast Mussels

Prep Time	Cook Time	Serving
5 Minutes	5 Minutes	4

Ingredients

1 yellow onion, chopped
1 radicchio, chopped
2 pounds mussels, scrubbed and debearded
1 pound baby spinach
1 garlic clove, minced
1 cup water
A drizzle of olive oil
A pinch of sea salt and black pepper

Directions

1.1. Set your instant pot on Sauté mode, add the oil, heat it up, add onion and garlic, stir and sauté them for 2 minutes.

2. Add water, salt and pepper, stir, add the steamer basket, place mussels inside, cover and cook on High for 3 minutes

3. Arrange spinach and radicchio on a platter, add mussels, drizzle the juices from the pot and serve.

Enjoy!

Nutrition:

calories 192, fat 2, fiber 1, carbs 2, protein 3

Sophia
SANDERSON

thank you for purchasing and reading my book.

is the result of many years of study, experience, harmony and passion,

we hope that the recipes have helped you color and embellish your tables.
if you liked this diet also try to take a look at my series of books.

leave a review if you like, can't wait to hear your feedback!
thanks again, regards, chef Sophia